Conte

For my children, family, and friends

Edited with the assistance of
Marnie Summerfield Smith
yourmemoir.co.uk
07710 721389
marnie@yourmemoir.co.uk

One

I WAS eight years old when a bomb first impacted my life. It was 1941, the so called phoney period of the Second World War was over and the Blitz was savaging London. I lived in Scylla Road, Peckham in south London – the borough in which I was born on May 12, 1933. I shared my home with my father Stephen, my mother Jenny, my older sister Jean and younger brothers, Peter and Kenneth.

Between September 1940 and May 1941, London was attacked 71 times with almost 50 bombs falling on Peckham. One destroyed our roof and blew out our windows making us homeless. We went first to a nearby community centre and then, quite quickly, we were evacuated to a lovely house in Shoreham by Sea in Sussex.

It was the second time I had been evacuated. The first time was not long after the war began. Jean and I were sent to live on a farm just outside Doncaster in Yorkshire. Peter and Ken were too young to go. It wasn't a very pleasant experience for us because although the woman had two children about our age she treated us incomers quite differently. Each morning we had eggs for breakfast but the family children got one each and Jean and I had to share.

"That's your ration," we were told.

Whether we had exactly half or Jean had the yolk and I had the white or vice versa I don't remember, but the overriding feeling expressed was that we were not family. We were in Yorkshire for about seven months.

My father, a heating and ventilation engineer who worked for GN Haden, was called up and served with the Royal Pioneer Corps, a combatant corps used for light engineering, until 1946. The pioneers often worked with the Royal Engineers and were responsible for transportation and stores as well as the construction of the Mulberry Harbours, the temporary and portable harbour used in the D-Day landings. I don't know if my father was involved in this work, as we never discussed it. The pioneers became the Royal Logistic Corps in 1993.

My father cared for us, and was encouraging but I didn't have the relationship with him that I have with my own children. I think that's because I've seen a bit more of the world than my father did. But he wasn't a bad father at all and I enjoyed seeing his relationship with my own children.

My mother's maiden name was Brown, and she came from a long line of Browns who ran a greengrocer business delivering in Greater London. Her father had a contract to deliver potatoes and vegetables to schools, which he did in an old Austin lorry. During the long summer holidays of 1945 and 1946 I did some work for him and recall having to crank start the lorry. That hurt when it kicked back.

Our parents met in Peckham which is where they married in 1929. Jean was born in 1932. I came along a year later, followed by Peter in 1934 and Ken in 1935. My mother was warm and loving but we knew our place and did what we were told – most of the time!

The house we were evacuated to was a semi-detached in Old Shoreham Road. We had a kitchen, a dining room and a front room in which there was a piano. My mother and her mother played it. Our grandmother had separated from her husband and lived with her daughter, our Aunt Doris, not far from where we were evacuated. We went into the front room on Sundays when the fire was lit and music was played. My mother also played the piano accordion. The only other time I was allowed to use the front room was as a place to study when I later attended technical college.

Upstairs in the house was a bathroom, a double bedroom for my parents, single rooms used by Jean and Ken and a room in the loft which Peter and I shared. The toilet that us boys were instructed to use was outside. Jean and my mother used the one in the bathroom.

Mr Matthews was our landlord. He was a very nice man who lived a few houses down from us. We did errands for him. Isn't it funny how some names stay in your brain and others are lost forever?

Shoreham was a great place for children. From our back garden ran paths to the Sussex Downs and various woodlands, our favourite being Steyning Woods about four miles away. Peter and I went to Victoria Road Primary about a mile away. Because the classrooms weren't big enough for local children as well as evacuees, we attended in the afternoons and local kids went in the afternoon. Whenever we weren't at school we were off exploring. Being the oldest boy, aged eight by then, I was the leader of our little gang of five, including our dog, Toby, a loveable mongrel. We became six when, nine months after one of my father's visits home, a little brother arrived. Francis was three when he began to join us on our jaunts during warm weather, his buggy well loaded with camping gear. We had a couple of old blankets for bedding but no specialised equipment. We wore our everyday clothes and huddled together at night for warmth, playing I-Spy and when it got dark, making up stories. Francis never wandered off and we were never in any kind of danger. I don't know how good a guard dog Toby would have turned out to be, but fortunately he was never tested.

Every good camp needs a den and we made a fantastic one from elderflower bush cuttings. Cut and pushed into the ground, these rooted and over the months leafed up very nicely. Food and a little heat came from a cooker I made from a jerry can. I drilled a circle of holes on one of the flat sides and when we wanted to cook, put carbide crystals and water inside. I closed the can tightly and lit the gas coming from the drilled circle. It was very effective. I learned how to do this from my father's bicycle lamps, which worked the same way. I was always interested in how things worked. I was the only one of my siblings who had a ticket to the library. I read as many books as I could. Eggs, bacon, baked beans and whatever my mother could spare were cooked on our jerry can cooker with Toby enjoying our leftovers and dog biscuits.

We couldn't wait for the weekend to arrive so that we could go off to camp. I don't know if anyone ever slept in our den while we weren't there but it was pleasing that it was never trashed. I don't know if you could leave such a thing today and expect to find it in the state you'd left it.

When I became a father I took my sons to show them this wood. It was completely cased in barbed wire, utterly changed. Maybe children can't, or don't like to, make those types of camps anymore, or maybe they just don't get the opportunity.

There was plenty to amuse us in the daytime. There was a water reservoir at the foot of Truleigh Hill where we went sledging; steep and smooth – no snow required. We made a sledge from a piece of corrugated iron folded back over at the front so that we didn't slip off, and slid down the hill for hours. Also at the reservoir we played hide and seek and competitive pebble skating until we were chased off by an irate worker. We got on well as a group and enjoyed ourselves playing in the River Adur, making canoes from discarded building materials, often losing them due to sinking or the current. We would walk along the railway track to Bramber station and from there to the ruins of Bramber Castle where one could roam without restriction, play imaginative games – all with no entrance fee. Near to where we lived was a pair of ruined cottages. We loved to explore the cellars which were accessible due to the floors having fallen in – probably not our safest game.

Not long after we moved to Sussex, Jean started at a girls' senior school in Southwick. She made friends there and with other girls in the village and as time went on became more reluctant to join in our activities. She had always been quite reluctant and was feminine in her ways, which was quite natural I suppose.

Many a day was spent camping, playing and exploring. We weren't a family who had cash for games or pocket money. Consequently, Mum didn't put her feet up while we were away. She took in washing and ironing from the local community and worked very hard in our garden too. Dig For Victory posters appeared across Shoreham and like many people Mum planted vegetables and kept chickens and rabbits. She also went a bit further and bought a pregnant goat from a local farmer. The kids, after they were born and weaned, were sold back to him.

We had to help Mum as much as we could and our jobs included walking Toby, turning the mangle, weeding the vegetable plot, feeding the animals, cleaning out their pens and hutches, milking the goat and searching for and digging up wild horseradish. This was then grated and put into vinegar and bottled in jars. Mum then either sold this to, or traded it with, the local butcher who presumably sold them to customers buying their beef ration. Everyone had to be registered with one of the Shoreham butchers. These were Alfred Snelling, Ted Harmsworth, Jack Shepherd and Evans and Upton. I don't know which was ours but I do know that we were rarely able to enjoy the horseradish although some of it (without vinegar) went into the stockpot that was always on the stove.

Two

OUR main source of information about the war was our neighbours. A daily newspaper was too costly and we only used our radio when we could afford to have the accumulator charged. When it was charged, we enjoyed listening to Dick Barton – Special Agent on the BBC Light programme, today's BBC Radio 2. We had no television. We occasionally went to the cinema, to Saturday matinees, where we sat in the cheapest seats. There we saw the Pathé newsreels and got more of an idea of what was going on. We also looked to the sky where there was plenty of activity such as the condensation trails of aircraft in the sky. For some weeks they were heading in all directions so we knew that something momentous was happening and the next day, Mum bought a newspaper. It was full of news of the Battle of Britain. Mum must have wondered how our father was doing, but we didn't even know which country he was in. Dad wrote the occasional letter which went through the censorship routine and bore black ink depletions. I wondered what was underneath.

Next to arrive in the skies above us was the doodlebug with its strange and ominous engine beat. Doodlebugs were few and far between because Sussex wasn't targeted by the Germans and the only ones that landed near us were what were called short-falls. That made them no less dangerous of course and one day while we were in the school playground one flew over our heads very low. The engine stopped and the Doodlebug halted, turned and began to glide to earth. Fortunately it exploded in the countryside about a mile away with us children too excited to think of the danger we had escaped. Another day, Peter and I walked the eleven miles to Brighton to see our grandmother. On our journey home we passed Southwick power station, which was close to the sea and flanked by the main coastal road and as we did so, we saw and heard noisy puffs of smoke in the air beyond the power station. It was light anti-aircraft battery being targeted at a low flying plane. The plane flew over the power station, the rattle of its machine guns firing as a bomb fell from it. The bomb, bullets and plane passed directly above us.

"Run home!" I shouted to Peter and we took off, sprinting all the way. We later learned that the plane missed its target of the power station and hit a laundry. This was the onset of the hit-and-run raids, 37 in Shoreham in total, and I would come to learn that the bomb that fell was 250kg.

At the front of our house was a road, and beyond that a low brick wall on the other side of which was a single track along which steam trains ran between Shoreham and Steyning and other villages. We would scout the track sides for coal that had dropped from trains and take it home for Mum to use on the fire.

Beyond the track was a bank running down to the River Adur on which Walrus amphibian aircraft were moored. The Walrus was an amphibious biplane, a reconnaissance aircraft, and was operated by the Fleet Air Arm and the Royal Navy. It could be catapult-launched from battleships and later, due to its ability to take off and land on water, it became a rescue aircraft for downed aircrew.

On the other side of the river was an airfield, home to a very active RAF fighter squadron which attracted nightly attention from enemy aircraft. Despite being only about half a mile away from the riverside airfield perimeter, and having some exciting nights during which we sheltered, not very comfortably, in an Anderson air raid shelter, we escaped damage or injury. Eventually, we got a bit complacent about the air raids and the Anderson became a place to store animal feed. We later got an indoor shelter, a Morrison, with a steel roof in which we spent some nights. It also made a good dining table!

In April 1944 the fighter squadron left the airfield and the Walruses left the river. In the weeks that followed, a number of strange looking craft arrived and were moored under camouflage nets suspended on scaffolding next to the old toll bridge. They looked like flat bottomed barges and we couldn't get close to them. In May, lengthy convoys of vehicles – some towing guns and all full of soldiers – filled nearby roads then slowly moved over the Norfolk Bridge that crossed the River Adur and went onto the airfield. They were mainly American troops and we didn't see much of them. We didn't think about these strange things going on around us.

Like most children we lived in the moment, and accepted what was happening. The only question we asked was, "What's for dinner, Mum?"

Then in early June, seemingly overnight, the strange craft and all the soldiers and vehicles disappeared, and on June 6, the skies were full of aircraft, some moving slower than others and towing gliders which hung a little lower than the planes themselves. All were travelling in the same direction, which was a fascinating sight. Later that day we learned of the invasion of Europe, known as the D-Day landings, and saw in the newspapers that the flat bottomed barges we'd seen were landing craft.

After that the airfield was used by aircraft in difficulty, those that had been damaged by enemy anti-aircraft fire or enemy fighters. One day an American Super Fortress crash landed and came to a rest over the end of the runway and almost into the river. It was very close to the toll bridge, a relic of the past that was closed to traffic. My brother and I, and some other youngsters, crossed it to look at the aircraft's remains and wonder how the crew were.

American forces were a source of wonderment to us children as we had never seen a black person before. At school, in preparation for a getting-to-know-you-visit by American servicemen we were taught to sing The Star Spangled Banner and John Brown's Body, which we sang with gusto for our guests. We were rewarded by generous gifts of chocolate, chewing gum and boiled sweets – treats that we hadn't enjoyed for some long years. Some Russian soldiers who had been German prisoners of war and repatriated through England were in the area for a few weeks. They befriended youngsters who were then asked to buy methylated spirit from the local chemist shop. The

Soviet troops drunk this as a substitute for vodka, long before the violet colouring agent was added to meths.

All in all, even though we were evacuated, we were still very close to the war. We didn't think about it at the time but I found it quite laughable later in life.

Three

I LEFT primary school and moved up to Middle Road Senior School for Boys two miles from my home. The journey there was exciting as the path wove through allotments where my friends and I found fragments of bombs and shells. We compared them but had to put them into the metal recycling bin on arrival at school.

I wasn't an outstanding scholar. I think I was what you call a late developer but I enjoyed the hands-on classes such as metal work and woodwork. I mainly enjoyed my school years for discovering my aptitude for running and boxing. My fitness was enhanced by running home for lunch and back to school for afternoon lessons, once more through the allotments but with no time to stop. My enjoyment of physical activity led me to join the Army Cadets, Naval Cadets and Air Training Corps, enjoying membership of all three at the same time when I was 12. I even progressed to becoming the bass drummer in the Naval Cadet band, perhaps only because I had the build and strength to carry it. From the age of about 13 I had a daily paper round and on Saturdays a job riding a trade bike delivering weekend meat joints for the local butcher. Both were paid jobs and my wages went into the family budget.

Another activity I enjoyed was fishing. In the River Adur, a little way upstream from the toll bridge, was a midstream sand bank which appeared as the tide fell. It was known locally as Flatfish Island and at low tide we played on it, watching for the water to rise to an uncomfortable level and then we waded to safety. I met a man there who told me about a sport known as pritching. Armed with a broom handle with a barbed spike on one end – usually made from a six inch nail – you walked around in the shallows about the island, about knee deep, placing your feet carefully until you stood on a flatfish. The spiked end of the stick would then be used to spear and lift the fish which was hung on a belt hook made of wire. It was a productive sport and we nearly always went home with fish for our supper. This pleased my mother as it cost the household budget nothing. We also made primitive canoes out of scrap materials in competition with other local boys, which was fun.

When I was 13, I heard about Shoreham Boys Club and as it was an opportunity for more physical activity, I joined. I became the Sussex under 14s 880 yard track champion and just before my 16th birthday I won the Southern Area Light Welterweight Boxing Championship. I ran in my boxing plimsolls until I was given some trainers as a present. About this time my sister enrolled as a student nurse and soon after this she left home and moved into nurses' accommodation.

As Victory in Europe was announced there were celebrations but I only have vague memories of these. Everyone was very relieved that the threat of doodlebugs and V2 rockets was at an end. We then had an anxious wait to learn whether our father would be demobbed or sent to the Middle East. Fortunately he came home in the spring of 1946. My parents had somehow bought the house we were living in so a return to London was out of the question. Dad returned to work at GN Haden and when I was 16 I joined the firm on a five-year apprenticeship. Each week I would spend one day at London Polytechnic College and a day and an evening at Brighton Technical College. I was studying for a City and Guilds in Heating, Ventilation and Refrigeration Engineering and a Higher National in Civil Engineering. Fortunately, Haden's had plenty of work in and around Sussex so I often trained on the same site as my father. I used the bus or train to get to work but where possible I used a bike I found on the local tip. I found the frame first then searched over some weeks for the wheels. I didn't have a saddle so I made one from an old tyre. It wasn't smart, I never painted it but I was in business and away I went. It worked and that was all I cared about. I've never been one to spend time making a car look beautiful. I don't see the point as long as it gets me from A to B.

In April 1949, the frigate HMS *Amethyst* was sailing up the Yangtze River to Nanjing to relieve HMS *Consort* and take on board diplomatic staff, British and Commonwealth citizens and their families who were in danger from the Chinese authorities, when it came under heavy gun fire from Chinese artillery batteries on the north bank and suffered damage and casualties, including the death of the captain, before running aground on a sand bar. Eventually, the ship was refloated and sailed on to Nanjing from where it made two attempts to sail down the Yangtze to open seas, but each time the artillery fire was so intense that the attempt had to be abandoned. Any attempt to relieve HMS *Amethyst* from the sea by other British warships also had to be abandoned for the same reason. Finally, during the night of July 31, 1949, HMS *Amethyst* steamed down the Yangtze at 19 knots, returning fire on the batteries and finally made the open sea and contact with the other vessels, where upon the acting captain sent the signal "Have rejoined the Fleet, God save the King". Forty-eight naval personnel had been killed. Later that year the event was celebrated at the Royal Command Performance at the London Palladium with a film show of the event, when, to the tune of Hearts of Oak, a contingent of Naval Cadets marched on to form files either side of the curtain centre which then opened and a large replica of the bows of the Amethyst came forward into view to much applause. I was fortunate to be one of the proud cadets on stage.

I left the cadets but stayed a member of the boys' club and continued to box and run for them. When I was 17, I became interested in cycling and my father gave me his sports bike. I became a competitive member of the Lancing Wheelers enjoying the 12-hour distance trials and hill climb competitions. My fitness was bolstered by us not having a car, or much money. I walked, ran or cycled or I didn't go. I was often without the return bus fare to Brighton Technical College so I would often go by bus in the morning then jog and walk home in my regular shoes; trainers were too expensive. It was 11 miles and quite character forming. We later moved to a house in Brighton, my parents having sold the Shoreham house. My mother started a bed-and-breakfast business but it wasn't successful so she enrolled as a State Registered Nurse, a job she continued until she retired.

My parents weren't together for long after the move to Brighton. I remember some arguments and then they divorced, with my father moving into a bedsit fairly close by. I was able to see him as much as I liked and I also saw him at work. When my father died, 25 years after the divorce, he still had a photograph of my mother in his wallet. He really loved her. My sister and I tried to get them back together and they even went to dinner a couple of times but it didn't work. I don't know what the grounds for divorce were but marriage was an increasingly common casualty of war with solicitors setting up dedicated departments to facilitate the divorces of service personnel. My mother remarried.

In 1952, having met June at a dance at which the Syd Lawrence Orchestra was playing, I was married. June worked as an accountant in a local brewery. I wasn't very experienced emotionally or sexually and it's fair to say that I didn't think deeply about marriage before I got into it, but I am pleased I married June as without her, I wouldn't have my sons Stephen and Gareth.

Four

"You're a blivet, what are you?"

"I'm a blivet, Corporal."

"And what's a blivet?"

"Two pounds of shit in a one pound bag."

It was August 1954 and I was doing my preliminary National Service training. I'd received my call-up papers on my 21st birthday. Birthday cards and call-up papers all in one day. It still makes me smile. I had been called up at 18 but I'd deferred so that I could finish my apprenticeship.

I was to report to the Royal Engineer training unit in Malvern where I would become a Sapper. This is a name given to all Royal Engineers regardless of rank. The phrase goes Once A Sapper, Always A Sapper. A Sap is a zigzag shaped trench that allows infantry to get close to enemy lines under stealth. They were invented and dug by Royal Engineers, earning them the nickname Sappers.

The journey to Malvern was slow and there were about 20 lads on board in the same position as me. When we arrived at Malvern the sergeant lined us up, did a roll call and ordered us onto an army lorry, which took us to the camp. There, our personal possessions were deposited in a timber hut which would be our home for the duration and we were marched to the camp barber for the traditional short back and sides.

What happened next was basically a "bang them into shape" sorting shop – a rude awakening to many, fortunately not me due to my fitness. I deplored the ignorance and rudeness shown by some as my attitude was very much, *Let's get it over with*. The days alternated between being very exciting to unbelievably boring, the idea being to turn us all into someone who would take orders without question. I was fine with that but because I was 21 and the eldest by some years, there was a presumption that I would not take kindly to such instruction, hence the Corporal calling me a blivet. Eighteen months later when I was a Sergeant in bomb disposal, we'd been out on a job and on the way back to our unit, I called into the Sergeant's unit in Farnborough to refuel our vehicles and sought out the Corporal to say hello. That felt good.

After a few weeks of sorting the wheat from the chaff everyone moved on to other units. Having taken aptitude tests by then, I was sent to the Royal Engineer Training Regiment near Farnborough for three months training as a combat engineer. The service had their own educational corps and the qualifications I had already meant that I didn't have to attend a lot of things, although I was given odd jobs to do instead – one of which was a week as an assistant in the camp butchery.

Once again, the weeks that followed were a mixture of exciting hard work and tedium. The attitude of the instructors was much the same as during initial training. One learned quickly not to react to the aggressive manner and insulting language of the training NCOs and as the eldest in my intake, I was the prime target for this. Eventually, as the training became more technical and intense, the attitude towards us became more relaxed and civilised.

June and I's first home was a flat in Kemptown but by the time I'd been called up we were renting a house. Both properties were close to my family home and my family were there to help her cope with being alone.

Sometimes in the evenings at Farnborough, we'd be busy in our barracks and get called out to cut the grass or perform some menial and humiliating task. I would hide up in the rafters to write a letter to June. I was never spotted. Being that bit older, I think I was only one of a handful of men in basic training who were married.

Overall, I was pleased to be doing something useful and the work made sense to me. There were no transferrable skills between my apprenticeship and army life except common sense, and I assumed that when my service was completed I would return to work as a qualified heating engineer.

At the end of the course most of us passed as a qualified Combat Engineer Class Three. In the Royal Engineers, trades are split into three layers: class three, two and one. To move between them required an intensive course of three months. I was accepted and proudly wore the blue lanyard of a qualified Royal Engineer.

Five

AFTER a short home leave, I proceeded to my unit, which was 35 Engineer Regiment of the British Army of the Rhine (BAOR) based in Osnabruck, Germany. I reported to the movements unit at Harwich and caught a ferry to the Hook of Holland, followed by a steam train that seemed to take days to finally reach Germany. I was astounded by the desolation and damage remaining from the war years. The railway line was often reduced to a single track surrounded by hundreds of bomb craters and when we finally arrived at Osnabruck we saw a locomotive lying above us in the skeletal girders of a burnt out station building. It had obviously been thrown up there by a bomb. The second thing we noticed was that it was bitterly cold. Even our boots froze.

The British Army of the Rhine was established as an occupying force after the First World War, disbanded, then reformed in 1944 to control ground forces for Operation Overlord better known as the Battle of Normandy, which began with the Normandy Landings. After the landings, British, Canadian and American forces advanced into Germany with the British Army occupying the north of the country. When the war ended the British Army group in place was renamed the British Army of the Rhine, which eventually came under NATO command and – no longer an occupation force – became responsible for the northern front from Hamburg to Kassel in the event of a Soviet invasion.

All our training seemed to be aimed toward countering the Soviet threat. There was a genuine threat of a land invasion by a Russian fast land army. A lot of time was spent on out-of-camp manoeuvres which were days, and much longer freezing nights, spent without winter clothing, sleeping bags or field tents as none of these were yet standard issue. We were shown how to fold two of the blankets from our beds into a multi layer sleeping bag. Unfortunately, the blankets weren't waterproof and on return to camp had to be put back on one's bed still wet.

In training to meet the Soviet threat each unit had a Readiness Deployment Area which was supposed to be kept secret. More often than not though, when we reached it in the early hours, we found the Soviet liaison team there waiting for us. The liaison teams lived in the British sector and had freedom to travel in military areas. Perhaps by being there they wished to show us that they knew of our so-called secret deployment plans. There was no physical contact and having made their presence known they quite often left. This wasn't confined to the Osnabruck area but happened throughout the BAOR area.

The army encouraged adventure training to keep us fit and encourage bonding and one opportunity on offer was a fortnight's winter skiing. I applied and was given a place on the army winter warfare training base in a mountainous and remote village named Winterburg, which was reached by a steam train. On arrival, the 12 of us were briefed on the niceties of skiing and shown our accommodation, which was pretty much a shack. We were then issued with a pair of skis and ski sticks and shown the slopes. We were given no other clothing or equipment and wore our regular boots and combat clothing.

The following morning after a breakfast of pre-packed tinned bacon, beans and bread, we were taken to the beginners' slopes of very gentle descents, shown how to put on our skis, the correct stance, and turning and balancing manoeuvres. Then we were launched! Fortunately, I found it reasonably easy. Perhaps this was due to my boxing experience where keeping one's balance was of paramount importance, but however it happened I became fairly competent by the end of week one.

For those who had progressed reasonably well the second week was spent on slopes accessed by a ski lift. The slopes were fairly steep and falls were plentiful but harmless. It was invigorating and I was eager to get in as many runs as possible. The two weeks passed quickly and enjoyably although it was tiring and after a hard day's skiing we went straight to bed without really socialising. It was back down to earth and back to the regiment in Osnabruck on the elderly steam train before we knew it. At this time I decided not to continue with my boxing. It wasn't cowardice, I was being sensible. I was a lightweight and while in Osnabruck if there was no one to fight in my category I'd be paired with someone in the next weight up and get a thumping.

During my time in Osnabruck a field quite close to the barracks was being converted into a sports field when a mass grave was discovered, around 2,000 dead in all. They were former Russian prisoners of war who had been used as labour in and around Osnabruck. All in all, I didn't like the place. There was a saying that even the Osnabruckers don't like Osnabruckers, and I could see why.

Six

URING my six months of BAOR service I was pleased to be promoted from Sapper (the equivalent of a Private) to Lance Corporal. I was becoming a leader and I also received a small pay increase – both of which were very pleasing. I then undertook Junior Non-Commissioned Officers' training and was posted to HQ Bomb Disposal Unit UK RE. The unit was based at Broadbridge Heath near Horsham in Sussex, not far from where I had been living while evacuated and 30 miles from the home June and I were renting.

I was told to report to the Regimental Sergeant Major and on my arrival I went to the guardroom and was told to go to RSM Skull's office. I was summoned inside where he looked up and barked, "Do you know my name?"

"Yes, Sir," I replied. "RSM Skull."

Glowering, he removed his service cap to reveal a completely bald and shiny head. This was my first taste of the bomb disposal sense of humour and it resulted in me doing my first week with the unit on extra duties.

The camp was the bomb disposal hub for the UK and quite large. There were Royal Engineers, the Navy and the former Royal Army Ammunition Corps (now the Logistics Corps) based there with differing responsibilities. The Ammunition Corps was responsible for ammunition, the Royal Engineers dealt with everything in the country that was above the high water mark and the Navy dealt with everything below. The RAF dealt with everything on their fields. Not that we wouldn't deal with an emergency below high water if we came across one, of course. Within bomb disposal was a headquarters' troop and three field troops. Each field troop was further divided into an HQ section and three field sections. I was second in command of a section.

This was a training post for me and I moved onto the Officers and Senior NCO's Bomb Disposal Course, learning alongside Americans and Germans from all services – men who had done the job during the war. It was an intensive course with much to learn, ranging from bomb and mine recognition, types of fuze, location of buried items and the art of using timber shafting to reach any buried bomb. We had a training ground where bombs were buried – our job being to find the bomb and its fuzes and render them safe.

Either on the training ground or out in the real world because someone had reported it, the rough position of each device was known but we still had to locate exact positioning. The way we did this was by creating five foot equilateral triangles of aluminium pipes around where the device was thought to be. We had a Dennis trailer fire pump that provided water with which we could ease the pipes into the ground. Then an Electrical Research Association machine (ERA) was used. The ERA detection unit had a probe, a tube which is about three feet long. This is connected to the control unit by an integrated cable and when the pipes were at the desired depth and the water hose disconnected, the probe was lowered into the pipes. Readings of distortions in the earth's magnetic field were taken at foot long intervals and recorded at the control unit, a metal box with three dials on top. I learned to take these readings and, using a conversion table, turn them into useful data, creating a graph which indicated where the device was. During the war years, a standard timber shaft was designed that could be erected and allow excavation of the area to take place safely. It was put together as the depth increased and was ideal for any strata. I used it throughout my service.

All bombs have a fuze or fuzes with a capsule of highly sensitive explosive known as a gaine screwed to its internal end. This in turn is fitted into the exploder pocket which is filled with less sensitive explosive than the gaine but more so than the main filling. The chain of events being: the fuze activated the gaine, which in turn activated the exploder pocket filling, which then caused the main filling to detonate – all in a micro second. The best analogy I have come up with is that you need a firelighter, kindling and matches to start a fire, with a bomb the fuze activating equals the matches, the gaine detonating the exploder pocket equals the kindling and the exploder pocket equals the fire lighter to cause the main filling to detonate.

Having shown a flair for the work, my post was made permanent. The unit controlled several furnished houses known as hirings. These were civilian houses rented from their owners by the MoD. June and I took a hiring in Hove. By road this was 20 miles from camp and took two hours by steam train and bus. I could have run it quicker but I was working too hard to consider it. Rapidly tiring of the journey I bought an old Rudge Whitworth TT 500cc motor cycle for the princely sum of £12. This cut the travel time to about 30 minutes, getting shorter as I learned to ride the beast safely.

Seven

IT is not general knowledge but during the early part of the Second World War, the mainland coast of Britain was extensively mined with B type C anti-tank and anti-personnel mines. These were designed to be activated by pressure from a vehicle or foot and were cake tin shaped metal containers holding 24lbs of cast TNT fitted with a simple firing device operated by pressure. Three million of these were laid from the West Country to the Yorkshire coast – any place considered to be a likely invasion landing spot. As the war moved on and the danger of the invasion of Britain had passed it became imperative that these mines were lifted and the beaches and other places declared safe.

The mines were mostly connected to each other by galvanised wire, the intention being to prevent them moving under the influence of the tides, winds and movement of beach materials. Unfortunately, having been subjected to these things for some years, the wires had rusted through and the mines had moved considerable distances destroying the laid pattern and usefulness of the minefield charts. In addition, in bad weather mines were dragged into the sea and spat out again onto the shore. Along the northern coast line they had been laid on beaches below cliffs. The cliffs had then eroded, burying the mines in deep debris. A further factor affecting the value of the minefield records was that many of the fields were laid in haste by people who didn't appreciate the need for accuracy. An example of this was when we were sent to clear a beach that had been laid with mines by Canadian soldiers in West Sussex. On arrival, we parked in a car park that had been built since the war and it was apparent that no mines could have been laid on the beach since it was completely rocky. Then one of the lads went up onto a wooded slope behind the car park to spend a penny and called me over – he'd found a mine. A search of the area revealed that the woodland had been mined instead of the beach and those laying the car park had been very fortunate. Clearing minefields became a very dangerous operation and what had been done to kill invading Germans was now increasingly killing bomb disposal personnel. One of the most well known losses was in Norfolk where 26 Sappers died. Two of them were from our unit and we went to get them and bring their bodies back. A memorial has been erected at Mundesley.

There was no safe way to make a mine harmless other than to detonate it. This we did with service explosives but first we used water jets mounted on Bren Gun carriers to wash away any soil or debris. The water didn't trigger an explosion because the mines needed weight from above rather than simply a disturbance. Twenty inches of sand is enough to support a man's weight and not trigger a mine, but I wouldn't like to test it. They were normally buried a foot deep. Even if they had gone off, that would have been a bonus and saved us a job. We operated the water jets from the safety of the inside of miniature armoured vehicles. Care was needed as mine fragments could travel up to 50 metres. Once the mine was totally visible, we approached and attached service explosive. This material, specially made for the forces, can be moulded into the shape needed and a primer inserted – similar to a booster in a bomb – in order to defuse something.

Many civilians wrongly assumed that ramshackle fences with small danger signs meant that there was no danger. In fact, in my opinion, the public seemed quite unaware that after a conflict finished, the debris – much of it highly dangerous – remained for many years. When I joined the unit, there were records of 2,000 suspected bombs that equated to 50 years of work, not including frequent call-outs for unexploded items which required an immediate response.

Shortly after qualifying I was sent to investigate a report of a mine on Shoreham beach. The object was behind a house on the shingle beach. When we found it, we saw that it wasn't a mine but a partially decomposed shell. The safest way of dealing with it was to destroy it using service explosives. I spoke to the nearby residents of two houses, asking them to open their beach-facing windows, as the explosion would cause a shockwave that would shatter them. I told them to stay in the front of the houses on the opposite side from the blast until they heard it. I prepared the charge, placed it on the shell, lit the fuze and retired behind a nearby wall. After the explosion I checked that the shell was destroyed and then told the residents that all was safe. As I turned to go to my vehicle a woman said, "How can one so young be so brave?"

It made my day and I came to the conclusion that I was enjoying my work and could see a future for me in the unit, so I signed on to serve as a regular soldier for 22 years – a decision I have never regretted.

Eight

MY FIRST bomb disposal deployment was as a Non-Commissioned Officer in charge of a section of 10 Sappers. Our task was to locate B Type C mines laid on Littlehampton beach. The tide of the sand and mud beach rose and fell about 10 feet and the River Adur ran alongside the beach behind a timber barrier. The river flowed at about six to eight knots so the beach had been subject to extremes of fast flows and channel storms in the river and sea, both caused by weather. Of course there was no map of where devices had been laid here, so we had to sweep the beach using a mine detector – a forerunner of the metal detector. Due to the tide we could only sweep for mines in the two hours between the tide going out and coming back in, what's known as the slack water period. Our working days consisted of conforming to the ebb and flow of the tide and sometimes it was possible to work two sets of tides in 24 hours, making for a very long day. After about six months at Littlehampton the beach was declared safe, or "reasonably safe", as the expression went. You can never be totally sure and six months later we had to go back because one mine had been washed in.

I was then promoted to Sergeant and posted to Number Two Bomb Disposal group based at Fort Widley. This was an old Palmerstone fort, overlooking Portsmouth. It had been built to withstand Napoleonic attacks and the former gun chambers had been converted to bedrooms and living space. This unit covered the whole of southern England and all reported bombs, mines and ordnance were dealt with by the crash crew which was on 30 minutes standby.

Records existed of more than 2,000 abandoned, unexploded bombs that for a variety of reasons were too difficult to make safe. Sometimes this was due to a high water table. When digging through the earth, we would hit water and need special equipment.

Unexploded bombs, or UXBs, were allocated a higher risk category as they were a danger to the lives of bomb disposal personnel. Category A meant that the bomb had to be dealt with regardless of risk because they threatened vital installations and transport links. Category B were those which could be left for the so-called safe period to enable clockwork and condenser fuzes to run down and Category C were those which could be left until time and operational conditions allowed the disposal teams to return to deal with them. Most abandoned bombs were in this category. Where possible, the positions of suspected bombs were recorded and the details kept in the HQ operations room, or ops room.

Many of the unit labourers were Ukrainian former prisoners of war who, after peace was declared, decided it was safer to remain working for the MoD than return to their homeland which was now under Soviet control. They were employed in sweeping for mines and digging shafts to reach buried UXBs. They were a good bunch and spoke English. I commanded a detachment of four soldiers and six labourers. Everyone on detachment lived in civilian accommodation that they found for themselves. Communication with the troop HQ was by a daily telephoned progress report and by post. The personal pay and living allowance was received by post addressed to the nearest post office.

On one occasion, having been briefed and given records of three unexploded bombs in Tonbridge, Kent we left Fort Widley in three 4-tonne vehicles, one for personnel and two containing equipment. The first bomb was buried in woods which were part of the Princess Christine estate at Hildenborough. This meant that fortunately there were no houses nearby.

Finding the site was comparatively easy as a shallow depression indicated a possible hole of entry but it took us three days to locate the UXB at a depth of 18 foot. The indications from our readings were that it was a 250kg bomb lying almost vertical. This type of bomb could be fitted with a variety of fuzes ranging from impact through clockwork delay to anti-handling, or a combination of two. The means of reaching buried bombs involved the use of a standard nine-by-eight foot timber shaft dug by hand with non-metallic tools. It is important to use these until the bomb is identified as not having a magnetic actuated fuze. The timber shaft was essentially pre-formed vetting that prevented collapse and it was inserted by hand as digging progressed. The timbers, known as runners, were lowered individually and secured using a system of wedges as each foot was dug out. It was hard work.

Excavation continued until at a depth of 12 feet the crumpled remains of a 250kg tail unit were uncovered confirming the size of the UXB and giving a clue as to its possible fuzing. As a bomb penetrates the ground, it leaves behind an area of disturbed soil equal to its diameter. This is known as the trace. In addition, a bomb often loses its tail as it goes through the ground and turns towards the surface before coming to a standstill. Work continued cautiously with the bomb's trace being probed for possible contact at 12 inch intervals. At 15 feet the probe made contact and a magnetic microphone was attached to the probe. This would remain in contact until the bomb was uncovered and a listening watch, a Sapper positioned in a safe area wearing a remote headphone set connected to the microphone in the ground, was set up. Careful digging then proceeded, taking five days to uncover the bomb. It was in perfect condition, lying almost vertical with the fuze uppermost. This was a bonus as most UXBs seemed to finish with the fuze underneath, which involved further digging or a hazardous rolling over of the bomb. Fortunately it had a 25 series fuze which was an impact fuze although a ZUS40 anti-withdrawal device could have been fitted under it. A ZUS40 cannot be seen from the outside of a bomb so it is impossible to know if it has been attached without the use of a radioactive camera. It became normal to immunise the fuze and either withdraw it by remote means or trepan the bomb casing and steam out the explosive filling then detonate the fuze or where possible detonate the bomb where it was.

HQ was informed and Major W Hartley GM arrived to immunise the fuze as an officer had to be present. When the fuze was immunised, the UXB was taken, with a police escort, to Fairlight Glen near Hastings, where a bomb disposal detachment were clearing a beach minefield. At low tide, the bomb was taken onto the sands then, when it was covered by the high tide, it was detonated. A high order detonation took place. This is a complete destruction of a bomb or missile and its filling and is by far the safest means of disposal as all of the dangerous components and the main filling are instantly destroyed. Immunising a fuze, which was followed by cutting a hole through the bomb casing and removing the main filling, still left you with the fuze in its exploder pocket with sensitive explosive booster pellets and the removed main filling to safely dispose of. In this situation the fuze and its pocket are destroyed by explosive detonation and the main fill by controlled burning. I found the work very satisfying and began to feel that what I was doing was serving my community and making it safer.

Nine

THERE was no shortage of UXBs to be made safe and having completed the task at Hildenborough we moved onto a hop field close to Tonbridge. The field was very hard clay and there was no water supply available to soften it. We requested HQ send us a mechanical drilling rig, called a Boyles rig. This had to be mounted on a platform constructed from Bailey bridging cribs and bomb disposal timber. Bailey bridge panels were about six feet long and four feet high. They could be secured to each other with bridging clips, a screw-type clamp. In this situation they were constructed to form a base on which to build a platform of shafting timbers on which the Boyles rig was mounted about eight feet above the ground surface. Incredibly, the motor which powered the rig was that which used to power the former Morris T model, mounted as such during the war years or soon after. It was old, but it did the job admirably. Progress was much slower than water jetting but after three weeks a graph had been formed that indicated a metallic object at about 16 feet.

Excavation started and proceeded for a further three weeks until the detached 50kg tail unit was found at 10 feet down. Another two feet down the soil resistance lessened. This indicated a possible camouflet – a cavity formed by a bomb that had exploded underground and left no trace of that at the surface. Such cavities can collapse without warning, and are usually filled with deadly carbon-monoxide gas, a breath of which can prove fatal. A bomb exploding underground saves a lot of effort and risk to life but you need proof that this is what has happened so, given the potential for deadly gas, digging continued cautiously with those in the shaft wearing life lines to the surface and watched by a safety rescue team. Another three feet down fragments of a detonated 50kg bomb were seen and removed, proving that the site was safe. The shaft was then backfilled, the timbers taken out, the Boyles rig returned to HQ, the site tidied and preparations made to move onto the next task at Riverhead near Seven Oaks. The gas would slowly dissipate.

At Riverhead the suspected UXB lay under a post-war road running through a housing estate, also built after the conflict. We broke the road surface by hand and the ERA showed a metallic object at about 20 feet. Standard shafting procedures were followed until, at a depth of 16 feet, fragments of an exploded 50kg bomb were recovered, an obvious camouflet, so we reported this to HQ and Sevenoaks council and backfilled the excavated shaft.

We returned to Fort Widley and while the team was deployed to a local clearance task, I accompanied the Troop Sergeant Major to Devon where relics of anti-tank traps, laid by the Home Guard, had been discovered. These consisted of 45 gallon oil drums filled with a flammable liquid known as Fougasse, dug into roadside banks usually at the top of an incline. Behind, and in contact with the drum, was an earthenware pipe down which a one pound gun cotton charge would be lowered and fired remotely as an enemy tank or vehicle attempted to pass by. The detonation would rupture the drum ends, which then became a barrel, forcing a dense spray of highly dangerous flaming liquid from the front of the drum 50 yards down the road to engulf the enemy. Fortunately, the explosive charges had not been fitted but the excavation of each drum followed by its removal to a suitable site for ignition using explosives was both arduous and dangerous. The effectiveness of this primitive weapon was proven when one which was leaking and too dangerous to move had to be activated where it lay. The resulting inferno left over 50 yards of a B road burnt through to its foundations and unusable until resurfaced. This did not make us popular with the authority responsible for the road.

Soon I was en route to a site near Barnstaple in Devon – Saunton Sands, which had become a post-war holiday resort. This was an area of beach and sand dunes along Barnstable Bay. It had been used by American troops training with live munitions in preparation for D-Day. This left many unexploded items behind, usually buried, and following several incidents and injuries to holiday makers the clearance became a matter of some urgency.

We reconnoitred the area and made a clearance plan. The sand dunes on the beach restricted visibility to 50 yards which made it difficult to ensure that no one was close by. This led to some embarrassing encounters as the dunes were also very popular with honeymooners and courting couples. Still, work progressed and a considerable number of 60mm US mortar bombs were found. These were detonated in piles of six either early in the morning or late in the evening when it was reasonable to assume that no one was about. Unfortunately, this resulted in complaints from the management of a nearby hotel who had already complained that our presence on the sands was harming their trade. I would have thought that having one of their guests getting injured on the beach would be more harmful, and that they should have been grateful. I didn't say anything of course.

During one of the clearance operations, a pile of bombs was prepared, the charge placed and, when the fuze was lit, we went behind the nearest sand dune. The detonation was loud and clear as was the sound of the fragments winging their way through the air. Above all that, however, was a screaming noise as an intact bomb was thrown off the pile by the explosion and tumbled noisily into the sky. Time stood still as the sound died, the object reached the peak of its trajectory and then increased again as it began its return to earth. I wished like never before that I had a head made of steel and the ability to shrink. A nearby thud announced the end of a frightening experience and we searched to find the remnants.

Demolitions of any kind required us to be vigilant about public safety, moving people to a safe distance and setting up a cordon. This seems a fairly simple exercise in flat, open country, but in rough or wooded areas you can't help thinking that someone may have been overlooked or wandered through a blind spot in the cordon.

Two mines had been located in the dunes in a lonely and remote area popular with courting couples. The mines could not be disarmed and were therefore to be blown up where they had been found. While the area was being cleared and the cordon established I busied myself making up the demolition charges and finding a safe spot to go to after the fuzes had been lit.

Having checked that the cordon was in place and the area cleared, I signalled demolition in two minutes and lit the fuze, retiring to my safe place from where I could overlook the demolition site. As I watched I was horrified to see a man in a bathing costume appear as if from nowhere and stroll across to see what was burning. Thoughts of a board of enquiry into a fatality lent speed to my heels, and I ran across the beach, gripped the man by the arm and dragged him back to where he had appeared from. Hushing his protests, and those of the two naked women who seemed to be his companions, I squatted down and explained the situation. This was given weight by a loud boom as the mines detonated. The trio were quite complacent and offered me a drink from their flask. The ladies' lack of clothing made the situation seem unreal. They had seen the soldiers searching the dunes and me working at the mines but had kept quiet because they were enjoying the sun. Curiosity overwhelmed the man and he became keen to have a look – presumably at the mines! After three months the area was considered safe and we returned to Fort Widley.

Unfortunately, soon after this, a group of seven schoolboys found a B Type C mine close to Lulworth Cove in Devon. To them it appeared to be a lidded tin that might contain items of interest and they were determined to open it. One of the seven expressed concern and backed away while the remaining six gathered around. The mine detonated killing all six boys and our deployment to the scene to search for more mines was a distressing experience. Like many service personnel, I would be seeing many more extremely disturbing scenes as the years progressed. Like many others I would develop a personal technique of putting them into a mental box and trying to keep its lid firmly shut.

Ten

ABOUT this time an SC1000 bomb was recovered and taken to Lydd ranges for a low order detonation. The SC1000 was a general purpose, thin cased, high explosive demolition bomb used by the Germans. Weighing more than 1,000kg it was nicknamed the Hermann by the Germans after the fat Luftwaffe commander Hermann Goring.

A low order detonation was when the casing of an UXB was penetrated with a small shaped charge. The charge was prepared and fired remotely by a disposal crew sheltering in a nearby bunker. On this occasion the charge didn't work and did not produce the desired effect of splitting the case and burning the main filling. On inspecting the bomb the Warrant Officer in charge noticed what appeared to be water seeping out of the small hole made by the shaped charge. He decided the bomb was full of water which he would vent from the casing using a charge of plastic explosive. A charge was made up and placed on the bomb. The squad went back into the bunker and the charge was detonated remotely. The results were catastrophic. The bomb completely exploded and the blast wave caused the bunker in which the men were sheltering to collapse, injured a Range Warden some three hundred yards away and shattered many sea facing windows in the nearby town of Lydd. Fortunately, the men in the collapsed bunker were able to free themselves having suffered minor injuries and equally fortunately, nobody in Lydd was injured by flying glass.

The water had in fact been nitro glycerine and the casual identification disastrous, especially as it was known that the Hermann bombs sometimes had a main filling of powder explosive which could deteriorate over time and turn into the oily, explosive liquid. Shortly after this the Warrant Officer was posted to a field squadron – his bomb disposal days were over.

During the war some large area targets for the Luftwaffe went dark at night, with nearby decoy areas lit up to mislead the enemy. These were remarkably successful in deluding the bomber crews and saved a lot of lives. After a spell of administrative duties on security, checking stores and maintaining equipment, we were deployed to Winfrith Heath, the decoy area for Southampton. A nuclear power station was going to be built there and the area needed clearing of unexploded bombs. Fortunately, the local strata consisted of a layer of loam with hard chalk starting at about three feet which meant that many of the UXBs would not have penetrated deeply and could be located using surface locators. The surface locator was a version of the ERA but mounted onto a frame with traps that fitted over one's shoulders and connected to the control unit by cable. It was swept side to side and able to measure distortion in the earth's magnetic field up to six feet down.

Having found accommodation on Matchams Estate close to Ringwood we started searching. Results came quickly with six 50kg UXBs located on the first day. Anything below 50kg is an anti-personnel device. All were quite shallow and easily excavated. Work progressed with unexploded bombs found and recovered daily, none of which proved to be fitted with anything other than impact fuzing which could be assumed to have time discharged electrical condensers. However, this assumption did not mean that the standard fuze discharge sequence was not carried out on each, after which they were transported to a nearby demolition site and destroyed using service explosives. It is never safe to assume that a fuze is safe although carrying out the discharge sequence meant that it was safe to transport the bomb without extracting the fuze, and was also good training.

Soon after Winfrith Heath, with my squad now numbering 20 Sappers, we were deployed to Glasgow, to locate a reported abandoned bomb on waste ground at Clydebank opposite the

John Brown shipyard. The location, scheduled for development, was within 40 yards of the Clyde canal. Due to the high water table the shaft we would create might flood and collapse so we took a de-watering plant and mobile crane with us, which is why I needed a bigger team.

When we located the bomb, we would lay a surface ring main of piping around it, but outside the shaft area. A number of small pipes would then be water jetted into the ground, alongside the ring main and down to a depth of about three feet below the suspected bomb. The pipes would then be connected to the ring main with couplings and the ring main itself connected to a wheeled, portable pump which would suck the water from the shaft area. Once started, the pump would have to run without stopping until the excavation had been dug, the UXB made safe, and the trench backfilled. Without this equipment, fines (tiny fragments) in the water would percolate into the shaft, weakening the support timbers.

It took two days to reach the site and a further day to find accommodation nearby. Clydebank council were very helpful in providing a defunct motor coach for use as a site office. Deployment was in late November and unfortunately that winter was to be the coldest for many years. Obviously the motor coach wasn't heated.

Having established that water for the jetting could be taken from the canal, we began. The cold was so intense that handling the pipes was painful. Even leather gloves froze to the damp pipes. You could remove your hand and leave the glove in place! A rough footpath used as a short cut by the workers employed at the nearby Singers machine factory ran along the edge of the site which brought many ribald comments from the ladies as they went to and from work.

It took three weeks before the graphs showed a metal object at a depth of 20 feet and we began to prepare for excavation. The dewatering ring main was laid out with water jetted to a depth of 25 feet. Probe contact was made with the object from about 10 feet but it was strange that no tail unit was found. It was at about this time that an official from the canal authority visited the site to express concern for the canal should the bomb explode and he insisted that I gave them warning of this. I tried to reassure him that it was our every intention that this would not happen. He wasn't convinced so, needing to get on and a tad irked but keeping a straight face, I promised that should the unexpected happen I would send them the detonation flash by registered post. This was accepted with thanks and they left the site! Some days later my Colonel received a letter complimenting me on my understanding attitude.

Work continued until we discovered that our bomb was actually a crane bucket that had been used in the canal's construction. We backfilled the shaft and left. In all, 240 pipes were used on that site and we explored to a depth of 30 feet over nearly four months. We returned to Widley, debriefed, and departed for one week home leave. The outcome was a success as it is just as important to prove that there is no bomb as it is to uncover and deal with one.

Having been very taken with Saunton Sands, I decided to take June there on holiday, having assured her that the area had always been clear. I asked my landlady not to mention our previous activities but on the second day of our holiday we were travelling by bus to the beach and as we passed the dunes a young voice behind us said, "Look, Mummy, isn't that where they found all of those mines and made the big bangs?" June was not amused and being pregnant at the time thought that I was being very cavalier with her safety and the safety of our unborn child. I would have thought it was safer for us to go to an area that I personally knew had been made safe, but there we go. I was pleased when a gale blew up that evening and lasted for the rest of the week, although it did also stop other holiday makers from enjoying the beach.

Eleven

I TOOK on the role of Reconnaissance Sergeant at this point which meant I would travel to wherever a bomb or suspicion of one was reported. I was sent to reconnoitre a bomb report that had been made by a woman living in a village near Halifax. This always involved questioning the informant regarding their personal knowledge of the incident. She replied emphatically to my questions that she had not heard anything falling, or heard a thud of something hitting the ground. Neither had she seen a hole in the ground the following morning. What she had seen, during the actual war of course, was a German bomber continually circling her house and had heard the bomb doors opening.

"He didn't do that for nothing, did he?" she asked me. I reassured her that there was no bomb or anything else dangerous and it became a classic recce report, much trotted out.

Another such task was in east London where the occupants of a house had reported intermittent ticking which they were certain came from an active bomb. As usual I went first to the local town hall to examine the Air Raid Precautions records to see if there was any record relating to the house. There was not so I went to the address and spoke to the elderly couple who had made the report. They did not have any knowledge of a bomb falling very near their home during the war but there was definitely occasional ticking, but only during windy weather. I asked if I could look in their back yard and on doing so noticed a slack cable running from the television aerial on the roof, down the external wall and into the house. I went back into the house and asked them to sit in that room whilst I went into the garden again. I gripped the cable and shook it as a wind would have done and then went back in where the couple excitedly said, "It was ticking again." Having explained and shown them what was causing the ticking I went on my way. My work was definitely a service to the community.

A part of the Devon coastline was permanently closed to the public as it was part of a military firing range's perimeter. This was not popular with walkers as it removed a significant length of a lovely coastal walk. Pressure grew to open the section but before this could happen, I was tasked to reconnoitre the area and produce a suggested route for the footpath with the instruction to make it as difficult to walk as possible. This was relatively easy to do as the ground was undulating and I included the steepest rises and falls into the route. After the route line was marked and fenced on the land side, it was opened. Unfortunately, dashing the hope that the rough going would deter walkers it instead became their favourite route!

We were called out late on a Sunday evening to an object that had been found on a beach and we arrived as it was getting dark. Identification was immediate – it was an unexpended flame candle float, a pyrotechnic device dropped by aircraft to mark a spot. It has a sealing disc that ruptures on impact with the sea. Water would cause the filling to ignite and give a visible flame. The candle float required no safe procedures and was put in the back of the Land Rover with the tools and the box of service explosive. As we drove away, we heard a loud popping sound and turned to see that the candle had spouted a flame. To this day I don't know how I got into the back of the Land Rover, but I was in and grabbing the candle and sprinting down the beach to throw it into the water before I knew it. The incident was easily explained. The sealing disc of the candle had ruptured as it was meant to but had been resealed by sand and dirt. The jolting of the vehicle had broken through this dirt seal and the filling, which when damp produces a gas which ignites spontaneously on contact with air, did exactly that. Jokes in the mess about torch bearing bomb disposers died away. Eventually.

Twelve

THE MALTA Fortress Squadron Royal Engineers had a bomb disposal troop which I was to join as the Bomb Disposal Troop Sergeant. Militarily, this was a single posting, in that I was going to meet my troop in Malta. Personally however, it was an accompanied posting meaning I could take my family. This was pleasing as my wife had not long given birth to our son Stephen and we thought that would mean less separation. Our passage was by troop ship SS Delwaria on which segregation of men and families was strictly enforced, so we said goodbye when we boarded in late November and met again in early December when the ship docked in Valletta harbour. Due to the time of year it was a rough journey including three days hove to – anchor dropped, to sit the weather out – in an infamous Bay of Biscay gale. Everyone was very seasick but somehow I escaped. The dining room was very empty – put it that way!

I reported to the Fortress Squadron Royal Engineers, which was based in Floriana Barracks on the outskirts of Valletta. Unfortunately, the person I was relieving had left for the UK several days beforehand so I didn't get a personal handover and briefing. This led to me being a little surprised to learn that incidents in North Africa were my remit as well as Malta. I was introduced to the unit and to the Bomb Disposal Troop by the UK Troop Commander. The troop consisted of 10 UK Sappers of varying rank, 20 Maltese Sappers, a Bomb Disposal Officer and me. I checked the specialist equipment and then went through the incident reports. There had been several fatal accidents and it was apparent that most incidents dealt with were a variety of anti-personnel bombs. Malta had been under constant siege by air with four years of round the clock air-raids by German and Italian air forces. They had dropped not only their own bombs but British, French and American bombs that they had captured during the desert campaigns. There would be a huge variety of UXBs for us to deal with.

When the North Africa front opened up three years into the Second World War, Malta, which was an Allied base, was strategically crucial with the air forces and navies of Fascist Italy and Nazi Germany fighting against the Royal Air Force and the Royal Navy. German Field Marshal Rommel said that without Malta, the Axis would lose control of North Africa. And so an attempt was made to bomb and starve the island into submission with 3,000 bombing raids carried out. The RAF defended the air space at great cost, but when the Axis began to concentrate on North Africa, Allied air and sea forces went on the attack sinking 230 Axis ships in 164 days, the highest Allied sinking rate of the war. For me, the myriad of bombs scattered about Malta increased my knowledge immensely.

There were no married quarters on Malta so at first we lived in a hotel in Valletta until a house became available three weeks later. It was a ground floor flat with a small garden complete with a banana tree, although we never ate them since we weren't sure when they were ripe, and also thought the owner might want them. Our home was in Sliema, about three miles from Floriana Barracks but convenient for local shops.

After settling in we quickly became used to the differences in life between the UK and Malta, the main one being the frequency of call-outs, many to deal with highly sensitive anti-personnel munitions ranging from the German SD2 Butterfly bomb to the equally infamous Italian AR4, known as the Thermos bomb because it was similar in shape to a Thermos flask. These were responsible for seven fatal accidents involving children during my three and a half year tour. They looked innocuous and people thought that since they hadn't gone off when dropped they were harmless. Actually they both had a fuzing system which had three settings: impact, timed and anti-handling with no way of telling which was set by looking at them. It was like roulette. We never defused Butterfly or Thermos bombs since we didn't know how it would be activated. The only option was to detonate them, as often the mere act of handling them would cause detonation or a reactivation of the fuze. I was aware of the first Butterfly bomb attack that had taken place in Grimsby in June 1943 when 3,000 of these devices floated quietly to earth. It was kept quiet at the time because it would have been great propaganda for the Germans. Grimsby was cut off and 114 people died. The Royal Engineers worked to clear them and make the area safe.

Often a call would come on a Sunday, the traditional day of rest for farmers on the island and it would become apparent that the UXB had been found during a working day and picked up and placed on a dry-stone wall to await a convenient (for the farmer) day to report it. Unfortunately, movement would often reactivate the fuze and the item, being seen by an unknowing person – often a curious child – would be picked up, sometimes with a fatal result.

Any fatal accident scene was visited by the duty magistrate and a relevant expert before being cleared. If it involved an explosion then I was called to attend. I stored these horrifying sights to the mental box that I kept firmly closed. Those who cannot do this may well develop Post Traumatic Stress Disorder.

One day I was called to where a young child had been killed in an explosion. It was a hot sunny day, a wonderful day to be alive, and the sight of a child's sandal complete with a foot near the badly mutilated corpse was devastating. Another victim of the Thermos bomb. The tragedy was unnecessary since it became obvious that the item had been uncovered during weekday ploughing and placed on the wall to await a Sunday call-out when no interruption to work would occur. Unfortunately, the child came along before the call could be made. I controlled my emotions whilst on site but at home I sat with my son and cried. Even today if someone is speaking of a gruesome happening, the lid on the box opens, I remember this child and struggle to remain composed.

The Malta Fortress Squadron, of which the Bomb Disposal Troop was a sub unit, moved from the barracks in Floriana to those over looking St George's Bay near Sliema. To mark the move it was decided to have a commemorative lunch in the Sergeants' mess on the final Friday. I was tasked with arranging the lunch and I arranged a menu of roast lamb and beef together with all the usual trimmings. It looked a delicious meal but unfortunately I was not aware of the Roman Catholic religious custom of meat free Fridays. In the event the ladies refused the meats but the Maltese men ate them saying that it was a greater sin to waste them.

The Bomb Disposal Troop was allocated offices, stores and an equipment bay used, up to our arrival, by the Royal Marine Special Boat Section. The outgoing officer said to me, "I'm glad your people got this office, I think there's a bomb out there."

What could I say, but "Thank you."

Investigation of this casual comment proved him to be correct. A 250kg bomb awaited our itchy fingers. The main building of St George's Barracks was on top of a short steep rise and below that was the office block, almost by the bay. Military families swam there. Explosives had been used to fragment the rock and make them a flat base to sit on – perks of the job! The bomb was in the slope and was speedily dealt with, appearing three days later painted and mounted as an adornment to the office entrance. Our standing in the unit took a remarkable rise as this was the first time the danger of our work involved the rest of the unit.

The Royal Navy also had a clearance team based on Manoel Island which was part of the Naval complex between Sliema and Valetta. They dealt with underwater UXBs and any on RN bases. I was astounded to learn that when they deployed from the island my team assumed their responsibilities. So off I went to their base to train as a shallow water diver. I did protest that I couldn't swim but was told, "That's all right, non swimmers make the best divers."

Whether this was said to reassure me, I don't know. All that time spent by the Adur as a child had not delivered. It was a tidal, cold, fast and dirty river and none of us had ever considered swimming in it.

The first thing I was to do was go to the RN diving school for an aptitude test. Those students who met the course criteria would be allowed to start the full course, those who did not meet the exacting entrance standards would not. I reported to the diving centre based on Manoel Island. Within minutes of arriving, having met my instructor CPO Willy Wieval, I was put into a flexible rubber suit and made to swim with flippers out to a Royal Naval Motor Fishing Vessel (MFV) which was moored about 100 metres off shore. From there I was to climb a rope ladder onto the deck. It was difficult but the suit was buoyant and I used my arms and flippers as best I could.

Once aboard the MFV, I was shown the oxygen rebreathing set which was put onto me by the supervising Petty Officer and his assistant. They tied a rope to the set and when I questioned it they replied, "We can afford to lose you but not the equipment."

Onto my feet went heavy boots with lead insoles and I was given one instruction, "If you don't like it pull the rope a couple of times."

I was then invited to jump from the deck into the sea. It seemed a long way down to the water for someone wearing lead boots who couldn't swim but my hesitation ended when the PO booted me up the rear. I'd been worried as to how I would get to the bottom: I needn't have been. The boots did their job and I was on the bottom in seconds.

Plunking around in the mud with water running into your suit quickly decides for one whether or not you'll continue with diving. After about 45 minutes I was hauled to the surface and told that I had passed the aptitude test. The leaking suit was a deliberate and important part of the test. There then followed six weeks of diving, mud runs – as it sounds, you run across the mud – and theoretical training. It was arduous and seemed to have been designed to make the Brown Job (a nickname for a member of the army) give up. It was all part of the inter service mickey taking.

But I enjoyed the course and passed as a shallow water diver using oxygen rebreathing equipment. As the Malta Fortress Squadron had no diving equipment the RN loaned us several oxygen diving kits which I used frequently to exercise my diving skills and when investigating underwater UXBs. After I got some experience I returned to Manoel Island to take, and pass, the RN free swimmers course which qualified me to dive below 30 metres using air. Over time I became involved in diving operations around Malta, Gozo, and along the North Africa coast, Tobruk, El-Adam, Benghazi and other places there. This was to become part of my bomb disposal responsibilities with incidents of unexploded bombs, torpedoes and anti-shipping mines.

I thoroughly enjoyed training and working with the navy and made many friends who I would meet at various times throughout my career. I continued service diving until 1983, attending various naval diving courses until I qualified at HMS *Vernon* (Portsmouth) as a Home Fleet clearance diver. This was great as I was the sole serving soldier who was qualified to wear the Fleet Clearance Diving Team tie. While there I attended a social event and a young diving officer who did not know me questioned my right to wear the tie. He was corrected by one of the divers I had worked with.

I was diving in the fairly murky waters of Sliema creek one day when, having finished, I began to return to the surface and saw out of the corner of my eye a gigantic jelly fish, six feet across. I nearly died of fright. Hastily, I returned to the depths to be safe while I took a better look and realised the beast was a large transparent plastic mattress cover that had been dumped in the creek. It had filled with water and was moving along with the current at about 12 feet below the surface. Harmless enough but it nearly made me have an accident!

Another not so enjoyable experience occurred when I was snorkelling 50 yards off shore to try and find a bomb. On my way back, a large surface pipe that was running across the beach and out into the sea began to pump out human excreta, used condoms and other distasteful objects. Unfortunately, the men who had been working on it had not been successful in clearing the pipe so they had used sledge hammers to break it, allowing the waste to flow into the sea. The only building in that immediate location was the single Wrens' quarters and it transpired that it was the sewerage pipe from there.

Thirteen

I WAS the Bomb Disposal Troop Sergeant. There was a field squadron consisting of a headquarters troop and three field troops of about 30 Sappers. This was similar to the UK units and the field troops were working separately around Malta. All the UK Sappers were in my team, the Bomb Disposal Troop consisting of 12 men.

In 1961, the squadron deployed to Libya for a month. The advance party went by air to sort out accommodation, and the remainder took the equipment by sea. The advance party established a harbour area about five kms from Tobruk, which quickly became known as Five Kilometre Camp. The squadron carried out various engineering projects and the Bomb Disposal Troop carried out mine clearance in an area where oil exploration was due to start. I'm not sure who was doing this, or funding us, but since there were no civilian companies that did bomb disposal, we had to get involved. We saw mines and munitions scattered close to the defensive trenches that were still there. There were far too many to dispose of individually but to leave them where they lay went against the ingrained principle of public safety so, being relatively safe to handle, they were collected and taken back to the unit harbour area. The toilet arrangements were deep trench latrines and I quietly dropped the day's haul into the Senior Non Commissioned Officers (SNCOs) latrine. I thought this was a good solution as the latrines were over six feet deep and would be backfilled before we left. I did this for several days without anyone noticing but then one of the Maltese sergeants found a cannon shell and came to me in camp asking what he should do with it. Not thinking, I told him my disposal method. There were pained looks all around, silence and for the next three days until the camp closed I would sit in solitary state on the box while watching a succession of the SNCOs trudging off into the desert with their shovels. I was definitely not their choice of a sanitary engineer.

We also dealt with several bombs and mines that were on the surface, British, Italian and German – all of which were used throughout the North African conflict and in the aerial assault on Malta. We were tasked to an underground water reservoir, made presumably to stop water evaporating in the heat, which the locals had been unable to draw their water from because they said that the retreating Axis forces had mined or booby trapped it. Access to it was through an 18 inch by 36 inch aperture near the bottom of a 10 foot deep pit, the bottom of which was swarming with cockroaches, which apparently lived by eating each other since I could see no other source of food.

I got a ladder and descended to reconnoitre the task ahead. I went through the hole and, feeling carefully for any mines, I estimated the reservoir to be about 60 feet long and 10 feet wide with a height of four feet. The bottom was covered in thick, smelly sludge in which we had to kneel and use a probe, one man at a time for an hour. This painstaking search went on for eight days and no mines or booby traps were found. The authority was informed and presumably the local tribe started using it again.

The next task came when a landing craft, used to transport stores, arrived in Tobruk harbour and inadvertently moored in an area where it was suspected there was something dangerous. Not surprisingly, the skipper refused to move it without assurances. The water was shallow with a gap of about three foot between the flat bottomed craft and the sandy harbour bed. Donning my diving equipment I started a search of the bed under the craft. This took about two hours. I found nothing but towards the end of the dive I noticed that the gap between the craft's bottom and the harbour bed had lessened considerably, so much so that my back-mounted air cylinders scraped against the craft's bottom. Having completed the search I surfaced, reported to the harbour master and returned to our harbour area. I knew that there are no tides as such in the Mediterranean but I did not know that there is a daily rise and fall of about two feet under the influence of the moon. Another lesson learned.

Another diving task was at El-Adam to find and recover lost engineering equipment dropped accidentally from a landing craft during an exercise. The depth varied from 15 to 60 feet and the equipment was found. While I was securing a recovery sling to the kit, I realised that I was being circled by some very large fish, I kept still as I recognized them as a shoal of barracuda. Fortunately, after a short time they swam off and the recovery was completed. As I surfaced, I told our guide and he laughed and said, "You be a lucky man." Apparently, barracuda are known to attack swimmers.

We cleared surface bombs and missiles from around El Alamein, which was a very labour intense task over less than a week. The ferocity of the battles that took place there were very apparent as the Allied and Axis trench lines were clearly visible and one could walk through where the major battles for the control of North Africa had taken place. These were ultimately won by General Montgomery and the Desert Rats.

While clearing a battle area near Bir Hakeim, the troop detected and uncovered 23 shells that I identified as being Italian 70mm shells. They had a green band which identified them as being filled with high explosive and fitted with nose time fuzes. The Sergeant Major of the unit to which we were attached disagreed with my identification and brought an Artillery Sergeant to back up his position. He agreed with the Sergeant Major's theory that the shells were British 25lb projectiles with a smoke-producing filling. There was no arguing to be done and the following afternoon the Sergeant Major and the Artillery Sergeant came to the site to see me destroy the items. Leaving two smug persons to enjoy a feeble puff of smoke that would signify their triumph over a mere bomb disposal expert, I retired with the team to the nearby protected firing point. Seconds later there was the characteristic crack of high explosive detonating and a whistling as red hot shards of metal pierced the air. Searching for the Sergeant Major and his colleague I found two pairs of heels protruding from underneath our one-ton truck. Magnanimous in vindication, I said nothing as I helped them to their feet.

Fourteen

AT THE end of the Squadron's stay in Libya the rear party was to fly from the RAF airfield at El-Adam and the remainder, including myself and the bomb disposal troop, was to travel by sea. On arrival in Malta we disembarked and returned with all the equipment to barracks; there we learned that the plane carrying the rear party had failed to leave the runway, over shot, hit the ground and burst into flames. Seventeen men of all ranks, including the English Bomb Disposal Officer and one RAF Sergeant, died. Most were from my troop and the officer's child had played with Stephen. I had experienced a strong feeling that I should go and see the wife of Captain Boatwright, one of the men who died in the crash. I did and discovered that I had had that feeling at the exact time the plane crashed.

I was extremely sad and went to visit the survivors who were very badly burnt and did not live. I have never forgotten what they looked like. The funerals of the local men were harrowing as the distressed relatives gave vent as the dead were interred in graves that had been carved into the rock many years before which, after a period of time, are emptied of the remaining bones which are then placed in a catacomb, to enable the grave to be reused.

The bodies of the British men were sent home. A reorganisation of the Squadron took place as some very senior NCOs were among the dead. I became the Bomb Disposal Officer and my tour was extended by nine months.

While in Malta, June fell pregnant and gave birth to our second son, Gareth. The call-outs continued almost daily and, understandably, my long absences from home caused some marital tensions. It was mainly my work in Africa that caused this as when I was in Malta I was at least home most nights. The boys were very young during our time there. They had other British children to play with as they got older and I remember that Stephen enjoyed being a cowboy. On one occasion we decided to have a family day on the beach at St Paul's Bay only to have this interrupted by a policeman who somehow knew where I was and came to get me to go to a suspected bomb. The busy life suited me but not my wife.

Periodically, the Cyrenaican state authorities asked us to deal with a bomb, which meant flights to their coastal region in the east of Libya and a stay over. There was a paid civilian Bomb Disposal Officer stationed in Tripoli but he seemed reluctant to get too involved when he had us to rely on. An unexploded 200kg Italian bomb was one such incident. It lay in an area where it could safely be disposed of by using service explosives to destroy it. About 200 metres from the bomb was a small hillock and the local expert wanted to stand on it and photograph the detonation using his new camera. I told him not to do that but he insisted and, as he was technically in charge, he had his way. A charge was prepared and positioned on the bomb. I retired to a safe area then, when he blew his whistle, I fired the charge. After the casing fragments had landed, I looked towards the hillock but could not see the expert. I hurried across to find him shaking with fright and holding his crushed camera. He had fallen on it when the violence of the detonation took him by surprise – an expensive reminder that bravado is not a substitute for experience.

While I was in Tripoli, engaged in bomb disposal for the Cyrenacia Defence Force, I was offered a job by the civilian officer responsible for the clearance of explosive ordnance. The salary was good and there was the offer of a subsidised flat, good insurance cover, and I would be on operation from a base in Tripoli. The offer was tempting and I decided to look into it. During my stay, the civilian officer showed me the employees he had and the various depots where he stored ordnance. All were typical. A fenced area of sandy waste about

800 yards square in which bombs, shells, mines and explosives lay everywhere with sand drifted up into the area and over the items. Walking around, I could feel items underfoot and many of them were in a dangerous condition having been attacked with hacksaws, chisels and hammers. No records existed of the type or quantity of the ordnance collected and there was no organised stacking. It was also obvious that the staff was under trained and my enthusiasm began to wane.

The civilian officer told me that in his security store there was a large quantity of TNT that had confiscated from local tribesmen. They had broken open mines they had found and extracted the explosive which they used for fishing. Some security! The Arab watchman moved a large stone and a length of wood from the store door. This fell outwards and down, presumably designed to fall on unsuspecting marauders. As I stepped over the door and into the store I saw a glistening, weeping mound of rotten explosive. Not daring to breath, I shook my head and backed out. I was beginning to see truth in the phrase, "Some fools have all the luck."

What made me decide not to take the job were two things. The first was when the civilian officer told me that he had gone to one of the depots to pay the Italian chargehand but he could not be seen. When questioned, the Arab watchman told him that some days previously the Italian had been working in the far corner of the depot. There had been an explosion and the watchman had not been to see if this was connected to the Italian's disappearance. The second factor was when I learned that although the insurance paid to any potential victim was good, the additional cover and payout to the firm was even better!

The Bomb Disposal Troop was called out on a number of occasions to clear small bombs and missiles from the typical Maltese wells. These were bell-bottom shaped, six feet across at the top, 15 to 20 feet across at the bottom and 15 feet deep. Each well contained assorted rubbish, scrap and muck all of which had to be carefully sorted through and then removed by hand to ensure no further explosive items were hidden. The wells also frequently contained large black snakes, sometimes up to eight feet in length. In the confined space,

with sudden movement unwise because of the explosive hazard, and sometimes impossible due to the clinging, slimy sediment, they often seemed much larger and possibly more aggressive than they really were. My Maltese soldiers frequently told me the story of St Paul. According to legend, he had been bitten by a snake and then blessed them so that all the snakes on Malta became, and remained, harmless. They swore their belief in the tale but it was noticeable they did not put their belief to the test.

After a number of these jobs, it became apparent that the word had spread that a cheap way of having a well cleared out and cleaned was merely to drop an unexploded item into it and report it to us through the local policeman. The time came when these reports were interfering with the many other calls upon our time and resources and we had to find a way to stop them.

Some days later we were called to an isolated house, which had been recently painted a gleaming white and proudly reflected the intense sunlight. The owners, a British naval officer and his wife, showed me to a well 10 yards from the building in the bottom of which was a deep layer of foul smelling mud and assorted rubbish. On the surface were two shiny 40mm shells, which could only have recently been dropped there. This was obviously another well cleaning job to be done on the cheap and presumably the officer had "borrowed" these from a ship. Tongue in cheek, I advised them that the items were too dangerous to move and would have to be detonated in situ. They could hardly contradict me and the couple were advised to move into the part of the building as far from the well as possible. After they went, the shells were removed from the well, put in a sandbag and taken, unseen, to a truck. A pound of plastic explosive was then buried deep in the revolting sludge at the bottom of the well.

The result was wonderful – a muffled bang, a puff of smoke and suddenly a mottled and evil smelling house where seconds before fresh paint had gleamed – the gases from the explosion having spread the contents of the well all over the front of the house. We were not the most popular people but word rapidly spread and there was a dramatic fall in shells found in wells.

Fifteen years later when serving as the senior military instructor at Marchwood, the Royal Engineers' Diving School, I attended a Clearance Officers' Dinner at HMS *Vernon*. Over the post-dinner port, a senior naval officer related his experience at the hands of a bomb disposal team in Malta which had left his newly acquired house covered in filth, although the term he used was much stronger. I decided that discretion was the better part of valour, sipped my port and remained silent.

The Rotunda of Mosta, or Mosta Dome, is a Roman Catholic church in Mosta, Malta. It is the fourth largest unsupported dome in the world and the third largest in Europe with an internal diameter of 122 feet and 30 feet thick walls, needed to support the dome. It took 30 years to build and is the ninth largest dome in the world. In April 1942, a 250kg Luftwaffe bomb pierced the dome (two others bounced off) and fell among a congregation of more than 300 awaiting early evening mass. It did not explode. Its replica is now on display at the back of the church under the words Il-Miraklu tal-Bomba – The Bomb Miracle. Although it was hailed as a miracle I suspect that the bomb had been dropped low and that the fuze had insufficient time to arm before impact and did not function. This aside, quite understandably the building is held in extremely high regard in Malta and this was on my mind when I was called to a suspected bomb there. On arrival I found an Italian AR4 anti-personnel bomb that can only safely be dealt with by high order detonation. It was only 20 feet away from the Rotunda and there was considerable concern among the clerics and locals when I explained what needed to happen. I assured them there would be no damage caused and felt totally confident in my ability. I had my men build a protective sandbag wall, shaped to direct the blast wave away from the Rotunda. This was an hour of being uncomfortably close to the bomb but when it was done and the charge was made up, we all moved to a safe place and the bomb was detonated. Happily the shaped wall worked well and there was no damage other than a small crater where the bomb had lain.

Fifteen

ONE memorable day in Malta, my troop and I took part in a large exercise that involved army units and the Civil Defence volunteer units, the idea of the exercise being immediate first aid, rescue and the evacuation of casualties arising from notional bombing raids by an equally notional enemy. Our role was to add realism to the proceedings by creating smoke, flashes and bangs associated with air raids and delay action bombs. The civil defence teams went about their allotted tasks with commendable enthusiasm and efficiency.

Suddenly, we had a real casualty for them to treat: a small explosive charge had gone off whilst I was holding it in my hand. It looked quite severe and felt even worse than it looked, so quite naturally I turned to the rescue and first aid party for assistance and the necessary equipment for emergency patching up, only to be told that all the impressive looking first aid packs were empty cardboard boxes, the contents having been left at their headquarters so that they wouldn't get dirty during the training!

I eventually left the site with a scarf wrapped around the injured hand. I was driven back to the medical centre where the doctor examined my hand. Having cleaned it he told me to lie on a wooden bench which had crucifix like supports for ones arms. He told me that he was going to stitch the wound then nodded at two medical attendants who were behind me. They stepped forward and held my shoulders and arms down while the doctor stitched my wounds without giving me a pain-killing injection. I don't know why this was

necessary but it was a painful experience to say the least. Life went on with me working with a plaster-protected hand.

We received an emergency call from the police station in Rabat, Malta about an unexploded bomb. Once there, we were escorted to a nearby house and shown into its courtyard, which was a cool, green haven from the summer sun. The UXB was an Italian anti-personnel bomb, partially buried in the shade of a lemon tree. Given that this type of bomb was designed to explode if touched or disturbed, it was not possible to move it without a very real danger of it killing the mover. The only safe disposal was to destroy it where it was using an explosive charge. The bomb was prepared for demolition, surrounding house holders warned and the occupants of the buildings around the courtyard moved to the side of the house furthest from the bomb. I checked the safety arrangements, lit the fuze and retired to the protection of the house. Suddenly, the lady of the house started to scream and wail. She had forgotten the family donkey which was stabled in an outhouse opening onto the courtyard. The unit had spent a considerable amount of time and effort on building up a good relationship with the Maltese public so as to encourage the normally reticent people to report known bombs, and the death of a donkey would definitely undo this. I grabbed a colleague and together we dashed through the house, across the courtyard and into the stable. Fortunately, the donkey was small and mild. Rapidly carrying, pushing and pulling it, we got it as far as the front room before the detonation. We were proud of our achievement, but the woman's gratitude stopped when she realised the donkey had given way to a natural expression of fright on hearing the explosion. From her pained looks I doubt that it would have been any worse if I had done it myself. Still, bomb safely gone and donkey saved – if not flooring – we had something to laugh about as we made our way back to camp.

On another call-out, I was shown into a semi-paved courtyard where the owner directed me towards the worrying object. In the shade of a bush something protruded from the ground. It looked very much like an arming vane with a dorsal fin attached but not quite like any I had come across before. I couldn't find it in any of my identification books. This was not altogether strange, as the Germans and Italians had dropped experimental bombs on the island, as well as Allied bombs captured in North Africa.

Careful thought was followed by very gentle and careful digging around the object using a trowel and a favourite tool of mine, used when extra care seemed to be necessary, a sharpened desert spoon which I filed into the shape of a small trowel. An hour later, with perspiration streaming off me, I realised the item was a bronze lightning conductor used to attract lightning and stop it hitting the house, essentially a spike set in concrete. I told the house owner and he remembered fitting it about 12 years previously but had never connected the conductor.

One fine sunny day we received a call from a police station about exposed anti-personnel bombs and as usual a vehicle, men and equipment were on their way within half an hour. On arrival, I identified seven extremely dangerous Butterfly Bombs and destroyed them all with service explosives. Back at the police station, an officious officer repeatedly spoke of the stupidity of souvenir hunters. When he stopped I asked him about the Butterfly Bomb that was wired to a shield, painted a nice shade of white, and hanging on the station wall. He explained that he had collected it during the war and as it had not gone off it must be safe. I pointed out that his patron saint had obviously been watching over him, reminded him of his previous outburst against collectors, and explained the complex fuzing of those bombs.

I could see that the point was going to have to be driven home so I evacuated the station and, creating a pulley system with a bent nail and long length of cord, lowered the bomb softly to the floor. Protected by the clearly defined disposal orders to destroy anti-personnel bombs in situ, I decided to detonate it within the station despite horrified objections. The bomb was screened using filled sandbags, leaving a gap in the bags to direct the explosion, and detonated. The resulting four foot hole through the wall and shattered windows clearly registered as we received nine calls within a week from police stations that had suddenly found bright, mounted souvenirs in their rear gardens. These sudden discoveries and the light patches their removal revealed on station walls were dealt with and noted without comment.

I was called out to another Butterfly Bomb and went through the usual procedure but the detonation did not destroy the bomb. I made up a second charge and as I approached the deadly object, something in me screamed, "Run!"

The sun and the world seemed to pick me up and carry me as I dived over a nearby wall just as the bomb exploded. I sat there quietly for a few moments thinking how wonderful the sky looked when my Corporal came over.

"That was a short length of fuze," he said, inferring that I had made a mistake. I showed him the charge and fuze still in my hand. The bomb was about to blow and I had escaped just in time, acting purely on gut instinct.

A task that I did not enjoy was when the reservoir at Ta' Qali collapsed leaving two workers trapped among the debris. The section officer and I responded to the call-out and carried out the search because we had ready access to explosives and diving equipment. Unfortunately, the missing men were possibly trapped under the fallen roof and probably under water and the task then became an engineering project in which we would play no part. I suggested that the wall be breached using explosives and a gap of about 20 feet wide be made and a standard army Bailey bridge built from interlocking six foot panels. This would allow a crane to operate from the bridge inside the reservoir. We left the site and some days later the remains of the two missing men were recovered.

Sixteen

THE SEAS are just as dangerous as land during wartime and anti-shipping mines were just one threat. An anti-shipping mine is a parachute mine that is dropped and goes to the bottom of the sea where, at a certain depth, it is armed by a hydrostatic switch. There is a magnetic unit beside the bomb fuze which reacts to the beat of the propeller. All wartime ships had propellers. When the ship sails over the bomb, it is activated and causes an explosion, which sends a large and powerful bubble to the water surface breaking the back of the ship. There were other, buoyant mines that had weighted cables that took them to the bottom and anchored them there. On the mines are five or six horns, each of which contained a firing switch which was wired to the mine's main charge detonator. A typical horn was about two inches in diameter and eight inches in length and if the ship hit a horn, and therefore the switch, it detonated the mine.

Working with the Royal Navy's clearance divers in Valletta Creek we helped recover an unexploded experimental torpedo that was wanted for research into the cause of the failure. The best thing to do with a torpedo is to explode it where it is, providing it won't cause any damage. Having recovered the torpedo and brought it ashore it was decided to remove the explosive filling by steaming it out leaving the mechanisms intact for examination. If the explosive is case solidified, which means that the bomb has been filled with a molten explosive which then sets inside the bomb casing, and you can get the base plate off, or cut a hole with a trepanner, apply steam to the explosive. Eventually it breaks down and becomes a solution with the condensed steam and flows out of the bomb. It takes a while but then you pick it up with a shovel and put it in sandbags.

On this occasion during the steaming, a small party collected the resolidified explosive and burnt it some distance away. My Maltese Corporal was feeding the explosive into the fire when, picking up a partially filled sandbag, he decided to burn the sandbag as well. There was a loud hissing noise which built into a scream and everyone disappeared in all directions with the exception of the Corporal who had jumped with shock, dropped his glasses and could not find them! The explosive in the bag had burned very close to detonation. Confined explosive will burn and as the pressure builds up more often than not will burn to detonation.

The incident proved two points, the first being that care must be exercised even with a porous sack wrapped around explosive and the second being the ability to "shift body, lad" that is, get a move on, when the occasion arose.

We ran awareness courses of one week for the island's Civil Defence teams. These seemed to be quite popular. The Maltese Civil Defence units were primarily, as were the UK units, created to support the authorities in a major incident. The one week course introduced them to service explosives and associated dangers and to surface searches for anti-personnel bombs.

During a free swimmer training dive (where you don't have a line to the surface) in Sliema Creek, I came across a considerable number of brass four-inch ammunition cases from shells that had been fired at enemy aircraft during the war and automatically ejected over the side of the ship into the water. Because the cases were in a pile it was obvious that the firing ship had been at anchor when attacked. The naval instructors were very pleased with the find and we combined to recover them then. When all of them, about 100, were brought to the surface, I was informed that such finds always belonged to the instructors who presumably sold them for scrap.

In my section there was a Welsh lad who invariably got himself, equipment or someone else into a tangle. Going to deal with a 250kg unexploded bomb close to Pieta Creek I put him where he could do no harm, in charge of the safety cordon with orders to let no one pass through it. Some 16 hours later when the job was completed and the cordon stood down he told me of the English Naval Officer who wanted to go through to his nearby home.

"No," the lad said.

"But I am…" said the officer.

"I don't give a bollocks what your name is, my sergeant said no one is to pass until he gives the all clear."

Two days later the unit received a well done letter from the Vice Admiral who was the Chief of Allied Staff Mediterranean thanking us for the work we had done on the bomb next to his home and complimenting the sentry on his devotion to duty.

The American fleet anchored in Valletta Creek on a show-the-flag visit and during their stay their marines embarked into landing craft, six of which swept at speed into St George's Bay which was overlooked by our unit. Seemingly without slowing the craft beached on the sandy shore much to the discomfort of those using the beach, then with great show the marines disembarked, complete with weapons and pennants, formed up and marched through our camp with much swagger while completely ignoring us. After about two hours they returned and embarked on their landing craft only to find that the water level had dropped as it did daily by about two foot and they were well aground and had to wait for some hours until the rise enabled them to refloat and return to their ship. My section where quite amused.

There has always been a certain degree of friendly animosity between the Royal Engineers and the Royal Artillery and one day I was called to an exploded bomb that had been uncovered in the Artillery camp at Ghajn Tuffieha, which was on the North West coast. On inspection it proved to be a Thermos Bomb laying in a flower bed in the centre of the gun park. The Commanding Officer was not overjoyed when I told him that it was too dangerous to move and would have to be detonated where it lay. Unfortunately the majority of the guns had been jacked down from their wheels onto the base mountings since some artillery guns are wheel mounted for transportation and use in the field. When they are returned to camp each is positioned over a base mounting, usually a concrete slab, and then jacked off the wheels and lowered onto the slab. Convincing him that to move them would generate vibrations that may cause the bomb to detonate was somewhat difficult until I told him that we had destroyed such a bomb within 30 yards of the famous Rotunda Dome at Mosta without causing any damage to it. We then had about 10 Gunners filling sandbags for us to make a protective wall around the bomb. My lads enjoyed being saved from filling and carrying sandbags. With a protective wall in place the Commanding Officer was asked to have his personnel leave the gun park for their safety. The charge was made up and the bomb detonated remotely. With the bomb safely disposed of with no damage to the guns, the Commanding Officer thanked us and said that his men would clear up the shredded bags and scattered sand for which we were grateful, and left to return to our unit.

An unusual task in Malta was the clearance of a British minefield which had been laid in the moat surrounding a Templar Fort at Id-Dwejra, not far from Mosta. It had been used as an ammunition depot during the war. The mines were the British Mark 6 anti-personnel mine which when triggered would be expelled from the barrel-like casing to explode at about waist height sending deadly fragments over a 50 yard radius. There was no detail of how many mines there were, or of the positions where they were laid. To complicate issues, the moat had become densely packed with years of uncontrolled vegetation growth and debris that had fallen from the ancient walls. Much hard work followed and considerable labour was expended in clearing shrub and rock falls without any mines being found. We tried to clear the vegetation by burning it but all we achieved was the inconvenience of working in charred greenage.

I was working alongside a Maltese Corporal, a steady person, and we were clearing a rock fall when he started to move round a boulder to get a better grip. As his foot went toward the ground I spotted what appeared to be a mine pistol. Prevention being better than cure, I swung a hefty push at him which resulted in my fist connecting with his ear, sending him flying. He was startled and angry but I pointed to the mine – the first of 36 we would find. Later he remarked it was doubtful which would have hurt him more, the mine or my fist! The mines were designed to be activated by a trip wire but these had rusted away, which was no help to us in finding them. Having cleared the moat of growth, rubble and mines, it was declared cleared and safe.

Seventeen

THE Sergeant Major's tour came to an end and his relief arrived from his previous post, which was an attachment to an Australian unit. Attachment to friendly forces was quite common and in this case the UK Sergeant Major would have been the Sergeant Major to an Australian engineering squadron. He was very confident and seemed to view the unit's personnel as lacking in some military matters, including dress, in particular the wearing of the floppy head gear designed to protect one from the sun. He decreed that they should be worn with one side pinned up similar to the Australian style. He himself wore his well starched and ironed hat that way. This was far from well received by the rank and file and when I tried to reason with him over this I was abruptly told to shut up and to comply. I reverted to wearing my beret and instructed the UK Sappers to do the same. A week later when all the squadron personnel, including the office workers, reported to the medical centre sick with alleged sunburned left ears I had a chuckle. The Sergeant Major learned about the men, and the Medical Officer ordered the rule be reversed and that hats should be worn floppy as intended.

The Pay Sergeant was South African and had lived in Malta for many years. He kept a bowl of raw chillies on his desk and throughout a working day would devour them all. During a conversation with him I mentioned his habit and was offered one, which I assumed to be mild. Wrong! It was red hot and I could not even chew it, let alone eat it. His habit had apparently, over time, destroyed his taste buds and nothing was now hot enough for him.

The UK members of the troop had acquired a pet Alsatian dog which was obedient and well behaved with them, but for some reason was aggressive toward the Maltese personnel. Maybe this was as a result of being treated badly by its previous owner, but we couldn't be sure. Ultimately, the aggression resulted in several local personnel being bitten and a few days after the last biting incident, the healthy dog became very ill and quickly died. The vet who examined the corpse explained that the dog had died as the result of blocked intestines. Apparently, a local custom toward unwanted or aggressive animals was to soak a piece of dry sponge in blood then dry it in the sun, making it shrivel, so a dog would think it was a piece of meat. When eaten it would swell in the moisture of the intestines and kill the animal. This made me absolutely furious.

Diving at an anchorage site in St George's Bay I was called from the water to go to an incident at a large construction site at St Andrew's. Without changing I went immediately and found a partially exposed 250kg bomb, one fuze visible with the tail drum distorted and jammed over the rear half of the UXB. What looked like a second fuze with a false fuze head fitted was also visible. False fuze heads were fitted to prevent the actual type being identified, which made disposal more difficult. I ordered an immediate evacuation of the site and returned to my unit. There I ordered the section to prepare, informed the local police so they could set up traffic diversions and returned to the site with a Corporal and emergency kit, leaving the lads to follow with the heavy plant.

On my return, I was horrified to see the workers working close to the bomb. The danger following the disturbance of any bomb is very real, particularly when it is a 250kg bomb to which, normally a clockwork fuze is fitted. These can restart on receiving a jolt and this bomb had been uncovered by a mechanical digger. I went to see the site foreman who informed me that he had placed two empty cement bags on the bomb to keep it from view and asked that we deal with the UXB later that night after the men had finished work for the day. I summoned up my best Anglo Saxon vocabulary, stressing the very real danger to all on the site, and the foreman, somewhat shaken, evacuated the site and was, at my request, escorted from the site himself by a policeman. It was not until later that I learned that he was the millionaire owner of the construction company. The job took its normal course; identification and immunisation of the two fuzes, casing trepanned to expose the filling, the cast filling steamed out, the solidified explosive collected for disposal by burning and finally the removal of fuzes by remote control. In all, the job took 16 hours. Wearily the lads cleaned the equipment ready to return to camp, and the defused bomb was loaded onto the truck and the site declared safe. The police lifted the traffic restrictions, I thanked them for their help and we left the site for camp. Back at camp the equipment and bomb had to be unloaded before we finished for the night. I gave a helping hand, the bomb swivelled and caught my thumb between it and a wall and finished my day to perfection. I had a sore head from the explosive fumes, a sore back and legs from working long hours, a sore thumb from the injury and sore throat through cursing.

Eighteen

WE CAME across an unusual situation when a workman repairing a roof in Floriana saw a Butterfly Bomb wedged in the guttering. Such an item must normally be detonated in situ but this was not possible, partly because of the damage to the roof and adjoining building but also because there was no way it could be surrounded with sandbags to prevent fragments endangering anyone within a 100 yard radius.

To clear the area would be a massive police operation so I decided that it would be lowered to the ground where it would be sandbagged and detonated. To free the bomb from the gutter I created a pulley system using two lengths of cord, loosely knotted around the extended arming rod, a clothes line pole on the flat roof, and the other around a guttering bracket. First, the bomb was pulled upwards and free from the guttering, then it was lowered and quickly encased with filled sandbags. The bomb was successfully destroyed and normality resumed. Unusual yes, but also successful.

A scuba diver reported a bomb underwater off Fort Benghisa fairly near the famous Blue Grotto – a major tourist attraction. I went with the naval team to investigate. It was good diving with excellent visibility and on the sea bed was a 500kg bomb which had two fuzes. It was decided to lift it using buoyancy bags, then to lash it to the side of our motorised diving launch, take it out to deep water and blow it up. It took an hour underwater to attach the bags and bring the bomb to the surface. We then motored into deep water, lit the fuze and dropped the bomb to fall to the bottom. It was now time for our launch to take us away from the immediate area and hove to in the clear. A fuze time of five minutes had been set and we had placed a "no diving or fishing" restriction in the area. A massive plume of water rose from the surface and the launch shuddered with the vibration – a job well done.

The airfield of Hal Far was above the Dingle Cliffs and the wartime means of disposing of UXBs, of which there were many, was to immunise the fuze and roll the intact bomb off the end of the runway and over the cliffs where they landed in deep water. It is now considered safer to leave them there rather than attempt to lift them to them make safe.

The Headquarters Fleet and Land Forces were situated in the fortress at Valletta and had been throughout the war. It was a majestic building with steps and mini landings linking the ground floor and those above. On each of the mini landings were 10-inch naval shells, one either side, dating from about 1870. These had been in place as decorations for many years, including throughout the war. One had to be moved during some restoration work and was moved by a local workman. It left a trail of black powder and as it was then realised that there might be some danger, the bomb disposal troop were tasked with removal and disposal. It was heavy work as each shell weighed about 200lbs and took three or four men to move them. With care, 10 shells were removed; each had an exploder pocket containing gunpowder inside, which is what had trailed across the floor. This was removed and the shells made ready for dumping at sea.

With my nearly four years of bomb disposal work on land and beneath the sea in Malta and North Africa coming to an end, I received details of my next posting, which was to Chatham in Kent where I would take a break from bomb disposal and join a combat engineering course to upgrade my qualifications. First, I was due to have three weeks' leave.

Before I left I was invited to go to sea for the day on a submarine that was testing acoustic torpedoes which were fired at a sound simulator at the base of a rocky outcrop known as Fiflia Island just off the mainland. The submerged submarine was manoeuvred into a firing position and a torpedo was fired. One could hear the thrum of its motors as it sped toward the target, then alarmingly the sound grew louder and louder until there was a thump as it struck the firing submarine. It had gone round in a loop and could be described as having returned like a boomerang. Quickly, the submarine was brought to the surface where the 20-foot long torpedo was found lodged between the periscope and adjacent fixtures. Thankfully it was not armed. We took a slow return on the surface and went into Valletta harbour where every ship sounded its horn and the crews lined the decks to laugh and jeer with typical naval humour. News travels fast by radio. That was my first and last trip ever in a submarine.

Three days before we were due to fly home a 250kg unexploded bomb was found during excavation work close to St Patrick's Barracks. On arrival at the site I found a police cordon in place, the site cleared of workers and the main coastal road closed. After a little careful digging the fuze was found on one side of the bomb and although it was not possible to identity its type due to corrosion, the microphone listening device proved that there was no active clockwork fuze. There followed over an hour of digging to ensure there was not a second fuze pocket toward the nose of the bomb, followed by half an hour of immunising the fuze. An immunisation set known as the "S" set was gradually developed during the war. It contains a bicycle pump, a hand drill, self-tapping needles or spigots, rubber tubing, a three-way valve, a pressure valve, a tin of lead-free lutin (a sealant) and a plastic container to hold the immunising agent. A small diameter hole was drilled through the fuze head close to the locking ring, a self-tapping needle screwed into the hole, which was then sealed with lutin. The tubing was then used to connect to the needle, the three-way valve, the container and the pump which was used to create a vacuum in the fuze and fuze pocket. When this was achieved the valve was turned to flow causing the agent to be drawn into the vacuum and therefore the fuze. After this the pump was applied to the hose to connect to the fuze via the pressure valve and hand pumped to a pressure of 25 psi (pounds per square inch). When this was done, you left the equipment and retired to a place of safety for 30 minutes after which it was assumed that the fuze had been discharged.

Then came the task of removing the main filling and destroying the fuze pocket together with the fuze. Fortunately, the base plate on the bottom of the device appeared to be loose and gentle tapping with a hammer and chisel got it moving. This saved the time consuming use of the trepanner, a grinding machine that is strapped onto a bomb and, operated by air, gradually makes its way through the bomb case while you're having a cup of tea. On this occasion, the base plate came off quickly and the main filling was identified as being cast explosive. The steam generator was moved into position and six hours of steaming and collecting followed. The fuze pocket was then fitted with an explosive charge and after warning the police, it was fired, and the site declared safe. The operation took nine hours and made a fitting finale to my tour in Malta. I was sad to leave Malta because I had a lot of responsibility there, dealing with 250kg bombs. What I had dealt with in Malta as a sergeant was far beyond my rank's responsibility. I hadn't known this. It was just the force of circumstances. Little did I know that back in the UK I would be restricted to handling a 1oz primer.

Nineteen

TWO DAYS later, my family and I were on our way to England. We found a flat in Hove, Sussex and made arrangements to stay there until I'd completed the upgrading course which made me a Combat Engineer Class One.

I became a Grade One Combat Engineer and a Grade One Bomb Disposal Engineer, which is as high as you can go. Combat engineering is building, mine sweeping, anything that needs doing in a combat area. Combat Engineer Three is training in using explosives, building bridges, both manufactured and improvised, mine laying and clearance and watermanship. This is training in working on and over water using military boats, rafts, ferries and motorised craft. Then you go on the upgrading course so by the time you come out of Combat Engineering One, your training in explosives alone has been a year.

When this was done, I would receive my next posting.

Three months of separation from Monday to Friday followed and after completing my course I was posted back to Osnabruck in Germany. It wasn't a place I would have chosen to return to, but there we go. For the first four months we lived in a second-rate hotel and then a married quarter became available. I was now an Engineer Field Troop Sergeant, in charge of a field troop of three field sections and a small HQ section, a total of about 40 Sappers.

Our regiment was part of a division with armoured vehicles so when they went out on exercise and required bridges to cross rivers, we built them. We also made rafts for river crossing and cleared mines that were inert but had been laid by exercising engineers as part of the exercise battle plan to impede armoured movement – still due to the threat of a land invasion from the Soviet Union. These field exercises took us out of barracks for two to three weeks.

Then in 1963 came the earthquake in Skopje, in today's Macedonia, which was then part of Yugoslavia.

The British government sent a detachment of Royal Engineers to build different size camps, some for 1,000 people and some for 2,000 people, and several schools. These were made from Nissen hutting, which is corrugated sheeting made into domes.

I commanded the advance party to Skopje, which meant a journey of 1,000 miles through Germany, Austria, Hungary and into Yugoslavia. There were 12 of us in four vehicles, taking it in turns to drive. The first night was interesting since we left Osnabruck in the dark using left-hand drive Land Rovers, which we hadn't test driven. Each night we stayed with party members who wined and dined us. It was quite an experience. I was given homemade Plum Brandy and learned a very interesting tradition. The first guest, which in this case was me, was given a tot of brandy as he stepped over the threshold. When the second guest came in, who was my interpreter, he was a given one tot and I was given two. When the third guest arrived, the interpreter's girlfriend, she was given a tot, her boyfriend was given two tots and I was given three. It took me a little by surprise but it did make for a very jolly party!

However, the mission did mean a four month separation from my wife and sons and I missed them, even though I felt overwhelmed by the work and was very tired.

The earthquake, on July 26, 1963, killed more than 1,000 people and left 200,000 without homes. Money, medicine, engineering, building teams and supplies came from 78 countries including the UK and the Soviet Union. There were 36 of us Royal Engineers. We made up five teams of six with another team in charge of stores and administration.

Each building site had about 100 locals who were hired by the local authorities to be used as labour. These reported on Monday morning, worked through to Saturday evening and then had Sunday at home. During the week they fared for themselves in or around the building sites. They were in the main amenable, though had little or no education, and didn't speak English. A couple in their twenties was stationed with us as interpreters and lived in a caravan.

We erected a flag pole at each building site and flew the Union Flag, raising it in the morning and lowering it at sunset as is customary in all British Army camps abroad. Within days we had taught the workers to take part in the traditional sunset ceremony, which they seemed to enjoy.

I developed a toothache and was directed by the local authority to an outdoor surgery where a female dentist operated in a clearing amid the surrounding debris. The dental treatment was good but after it had finished I was instructed to drop my trousers to receive an anti-infection injection.

There were aid agencies of many nationalities helping Skopje and the overriding impression we gained was that many of the resources were being wasted through ignorance, misuse or neglect. This was so much the case that when one of my corporals was being interviewed for BBC television and asked if he had made a contribution to the appeal, he replied that he had. Then, when asked what he thought after seeing the aid efforts he said, "I would like my five pounds back." Unfortunately most of us agreed with him. For example, heating equipment and pipes were sent out but the threading was imperial sized and metric was required. It could be used easily in camps under construction but not easily elsewhere so I think it went to waste. Rotary Club caravans delivered donations given in response to the BBC appeal, but as far as I know, those were sold.

The Soviet Army was also helping in Skopje and had an engineering unit whose role was the repair or replacement of damaged roads and bridges. Their work was superb and very impressive. There was little contact with them on an informal basis, which was regrettable but understandable, given that we were undertaking exercises in Osnabruck due to a real possibility of a war with them.

It's fascinating how on the one hand this tension was real, and on the other, we could all come together to help Skopje. It reinforced my view that for the most part, war is futile.

After we had been in Skopje for two months, an American engineer unit arrived by train complete with a band. I don't know if this was to boost morale. I didn't get to hear it myself, so I couldn't say if it worked.

The unit was 100 strong and they had superb camp equipment such as air-conditioned tents, magnificent kitchen utilities and fresh food flown in daily from their base in Germany. It made us with our standard army tents, Hydroburner cookers that run on a mixture of fuel, mostly standard tinned rations, water from a hand pump, cold showers and deep trench latrine seem poverty stricken.

During this time, President Kennedy was assassinated and several of us went to the US camp to offer condolences. It was then that I began to understand the deep divisions within American society, as the response we got was that he probably asked for it. They were quite difficult to get to know, the Americans. At least that was the impression I got from the Kennedy experience.

Our construction of two camps and four schools was nearing completion and we were able to enjoy the area by walking on the hills above a reservoir.

It was spring and early summer while we were there and the weather was good. The sides were 200 feet high and had paths cut into them. I enjoyed having a break. I was invited by the interpreters to stay with a local family for the weekend. They were charming company. I took gifts such as boxes of army toilet paper which was shiny one side, dull the other and nicknamed scrape and polish, and chocolate for the children, though there weren't any in this particular family. I think I took some army rations too. The toilet paper seems like an unusual gift, I admit, but people were in a difficult situation.

Tito was the Yugoslav leader who died in 1980, although he was ill while we were there, having just had a leg amputated. I think they were trying to keep him alive so that the country didn't dissolve into chaos, which unfortunately, it later did. During the Second World War, Tito was the leader of the partisans, or resistance, in occupied Europe, and supreme commander of the Yugoslav People's Army. Although he was criticised as authoritarian, he was popular and a unifying figure; a benevolent dictator some have said, defying the Soviets and definitely a controversial figure.

When we were due to return to the regiment in Germany our camp was dismantled and we spent several days as guests of the Americans where unfortunately, on drinking their purified water, and eating the rich food, most of us suffered upset stomachs. Fortunately we, and our Land Rovers and equipment, didn't have to go back to Osnabruck by road and were flown by an RAF troop plane to RAF Gutersloh just 40 miles from our barracks. Once back, we went on two weeks' leave and I was reunited with my family. It was much warmer than the first time I visited Osnabruck as this time we were in a flat with excellent central heating

Twenty

AFTER two months back in Osnabruck on various field exercises, I was told that I was being posted to Kiel in the northern German state of Schleswig-Holstein on the shore of the Baltic. I was promoted to Warrant Officer, meaning I would hold a warrant from the Queen – a very old tradition – and I was to form a combat engineer diving school. The site was shared with the British Kiel Yacht Club which was inside the German naval base, Kiel Holtenau.

The post was unaccompanied so my wife and sons returned to England and a flat in the Seven Dials area of Brighton. In a way, it was a relief not to have them with me. The two boys were at school and my hours were long and I would be doing a lot of night diving, so contact with my wife and children would have been very restricted. There weren't any other wives out there to keep June company, so it would have been miserable for her.

The diving school was to have a team of six instructors drawn from regimental diving teams, selection being based on qualifications and experience. Some of the men I knew from previous diving experiences. We also had a quartermaster, who looked after the stores.

The course we ran would be attended by all regimental diving teams to learn water crossing reconnaissance and the location and clearance of underwater mines, explosive charges, demolitions and similar. The divers came from all engineering regiments across the Rhine and there was an engineering regiment in each brigade with armoured engineers. Each regiment had a diving team but they needed the experience of explosives and clearing and laying of mines, thus enabling safe passage of vehicles across rivers and so on.

I was selected because of my experience in Malta and I insisted that the instructors formed permanent diving pairs as this gave them the opportunity to gradually anticipate each other's movements and, after a while, each other's thoughts. It formed a valuable bond which proved the method beyond any doubt. I also had a partner for all diving. He was called Gary and to him and the team I was known as Boss, unless we had an official visit when we would revert to official ranks.

It was common sense to work in partnership really. When you've been diving for a while, even in no visibility, you can see but with your fingertips. When you touch metal, your fingers become your eyes and you can tell whether something is steel or similar. You get used to each other's actions and start to read each other's thoughts. It worked well.

Each of the courses we ran took three weeks for 20 trainees who qualified as combat engineer divers. After a short time the Canadian Army diving teams began to attend our courses.

It was freezing cold, so we were issued with rum in one gallon earthenware bottles. It was 100 per cent proof. When a diver came out of the freezing water, he was given a tot, which is about a single measure – standard army issue in cold weather. We'd put a cork into the receptacle to take up some of the space so that we had some spare rum for our parties.

Physical fitness was mandatory with daily runs of five miles culminating with a suited swim. Being that we were on a German naval base, our run took us past the Germans' guard room and from the looks on their faces, I think they thought we were mad.

We had a sea-going diving launch which had been shipped from England to Hamburg port from where it was motored up the Kiel Canal to Kiel. The coxswain was the captain of the launch and also drove it, enabling us to leave the harbour and dive at differing sites around the Baltic. He was also a diving instructor.

We had dry suits for the students but after six months I convinced headquarters to give us a cash allowance for made-to-measure wetsuits by a general diving equipment supplier in Eckernforde. These were much easier to swim and dive in and easier to put on and take off by yourself whereas you needed two of you to put a dry suit on and take it off. The water flooded into a wetsuit and was warmed by your body but the first thing to do was to have a pee in your suit. It sounds disgusting but it warmed you up.

In the winter the sea froze and all diving took place in the harbour. We made holes in the ice with service explosives. In the summer, long after the ice had melted, a constant reminder of winter was that the bottom few feet of water was semi-solid and painfully cold.

We often dived in inland waters and having made contact with the German Pioneer Battalion at Rendsburg frequently dived with their divers and also went on joint exercises and shared social events. One shared exercise was in Bavaria. When HQ BAOR said that they did not have the means of flying us there the German engineers said they would help and on the day of departure we loaded our vehicles and equipment on a German transport plane. On the side they had painted a Union Flag. It was very nice of them and showed how close we had become within 20 years of the Second World War.

There was an engineer battalion on field exercises in a harbour area which they had established and needed to defend. When I went to the briefing, I was asked if we would act as the enemy. Having noticed a fairly shallow drainage ditch running up to and alongside the harbour area, I decided that we would wear our diving suits and crawl up the ditch into the area. The team was five strong, including me, and each had a thunder flash, like a large firework that simulates a grenade burst. The plan, which I didn't consider that unusual – only common sense – worked well and took us unobserved through their defences until we were alongside the harbour area then we left the ditch and placed the thunder flashes under the wheels of various vehicles. Each having done this, we returned to the ditch and crawled away unseen leaving mayhem behind us as the thunder flashes detonated. The next day at the exercise debriefing I was asked if we were Special Services trained and gained the impression that we were not the flavour of the month. I don't know why. We'd helped them realise that they weren't defending their harbour very well.

It was a rugged life. We worked extremely hard, were supremely fit and in our off duty moments played as hard as we worked. The divers' club parties were popular for the relatively relaxed atmosphere, congenial company and freely flowing drink, which was a mixture of vodka, rum and wine or whatever else was to hand. We often had guests from visiting ships and units of various nations. During one party I was standing at the bar with my contemporaries, the hospitality had been lavish and we were pleasantly plonked. The band was playing loudly and couples were dancing quite feverishly to the beat. There was a tug on my arm and I turned to see an attractive woman.

"Excuse me," she said in her American drawl, "Do you shag?"

At first the directness of her approach startled me. Then, no doubt assisted by the beverages I had drunk, offended me. Drawing myself up to my full height I replied, in a manner that can only be described as pious Victorian pomposity, "Madam, I make love, have intercourse and sometimes have been known to fuck, but I never *ever* shag."

Looking somewhat startled, she walked away and I returned to my drink and companions. A few minutes later a young American sailor came across to the bar and said, "Excuse me, Sir. Do you realise that to shag in our language means to jive?"

I thanked him and felt a little stupid. Later, I spoke to the lady and we apologised to each other, had a laugh, and a dance.

Twenty One

THE fast-flowing River Weser was much used by engineer units to exercise bridging skills. During one such exercise we were tasked to attack a floating pontoon bridge that was to be constructed about 10 miles upstream from Hamelin. I, together with the instructional team, deployed to a location about three miles upstream from the bridging site where, having covertly observed it, I briefed the team on the attack. Each of us would have carry a thunder flash, water proofed by being sealed in a condom. We would be spaced out across the river and using the current and flippers, known as fins, each of us would go to a pontoon, extract the thunder flash from the condom, ignite it and place it onto the pontoon before passing through to a location downstream where our driver was waiting. We would come ashore and go back to our harbour area.

The attack went according to plan and the bridge declared unusable by the umpires. The only mistake we made was that we didn't realise until we were holding onto the pontoon with one hand and using the other to hold the thunder flash, the only way to open the condom was with our teeth. The condoms were lubricated, so this was unpleasant.

Several days later we were tasked to attack another pontoon bridge that was being built. After a covert observation I decided that to repeat the previous attack was impossible. Coils of barbed wire had been stretched across the river ready to ensnare surface swimmers. However, as the bridge building process relies on the use of a crane, I decided that an attack on the assembly area would be the best option.

I briefed the team of six who, once again, were armed with thunder flashes. The plan was to go downstream together, come ashore upstream of the bridge, and using a hedgerow as cover, approach as close as possible to the assembly area then launch a surprise attack on the crane and remaining pontoons as the main targets. After this we would make our way over land to where our driver would be waiting. Again the attack was a success. Shortly after this, the exercise came to an end and we returned to Kiel.

On several occasions we assisted the police in recovering bodies from local waters. One was a young man who had been canoeing upstream of a weir when he capsized and was swept over it. Unfortunately, he wasn't wearing suitable clothing or a life jacket, which might have saved his life. Another was a woman wearing Wellington boots which she had filled with pebbles, presumably to carry her down. She had jumped off the end of a ferry jetty. Another recovery occurred when, during a NATO exercise, a parachute drop ended with two parachutists landing in the Kiel Canal where they drowned, possibly dragged down by their equipment. Once the bodies were recovered, we had to get the weapons and other equipment. The canal was 300 metres wide and more than 20 deep. It was not possible to stop the shipping traffic so we got the ships' timings and dove between their movements for three days until we had recovered everything.

During this time the Royal Yacht Bloodhound, skippered by Prince Phillip, came into the club's anchorage and hit a sandbank. It was feared that the keel, which keeps the ship upright in the water, had been dislodged or damaged. We went down to have a look and discovered that there was a three-inch gap between the sole plate, that keeps the keel in place, and the yacht itself. This we filled, underwater, using cement mixed with resin which would do until the yacht was able to be brought ashore.

Later, at the diving school, we helped a distressed sailing yacht owner who came to ask for help locating and recovering his vessel. It had sunk in the Baltic, half a mile off shore in about 30 feet of water. I decided that this would be an ideal exercise for the team. We loaded the necessary equipment onto the diving launch and motored to the location, which was fortunately approximately marked by a buoy. A quick search dive located the yacht, which was sitting upright on the bottom and appeared undamaged. I could see which fixtures the four buoyancy bags could be safely secured to so I briefed the team, who would dive in pairs and attach buoyancy bags. When this was done they would give the signal by rope and simultaneously the supervisors would open the air cylinders to inflate the buoyancy bags, leaving the divers to come to the surface and aboard the launch.

Everything went as planned and as the divers came aboard the slowly inflating buoyancy bags lifted the yacht until it broke the surface. A towing line was then connected to the bows of the yacht and the stern of the diving launch and we made our way to the marina where the yacht was usually moored.

Once in the marina, we took the yacht to where the marina crane could lift it. We helped with positioning the lifting strops and recovered our buoyancy bags. We backed our diving launch out of the way and watched as the lift began. I was surprised that no attempt was being made to drain the considerable weight of water from the yacht, and 10 feet above the water, the lifting strops broke and the yacht crashed onto the water and broke into pieces. It was a dreadful mistake by the marina operatives but a good diving exercise for the team.

One of our responsibilities was riverbed reconnaissance for an armoured division. They required a shallow, firm crossing from bank to bank that could be used without the need for bridging. One exercise was over 10 days and we, together with the armoured unit, were harboured in a wooded area. The armoured unit had erected a large tent in which they held a full mess dinner. This was an annual and traditional event which they decided not to forgo even though they were in the field. It included the regimental silver and the officers dressed in full mess uniforms – obviously a celebration of a day special to them. My lads, not to be outdone, spread a towel, together with a knife and fork, over a tree stump and told me to sit there. Then, with towels draped over their arms, they acted as waiters bringing my meal of rations with ceremonial flair, much to the amusement of the other soldiers nearby.

We were still in Germany in 1966 and had the joy of being English supporters when England defeated Germany in the World Cup final. We were living in the heart of a German service community who did not seem to mind our excessive celebrations.

Twenty Two

AFTER the Second World War, Germany was divided into various zones of occupation, British, American and Russian among them. In the midst of my time at the school, during 1965, a diving school team needed to be flown by the RAF into Berlin. A Soviet fighter jet of the latest design had crashed into the river Havel in the British sector and this was of much interest to British Intelligence who wanted the remains – especially the electronic equipment, the flight Black Box and one of the two engines – salvaged. I was to lead the team.

The Havel, at the point where the plane crashed, was about 16 feet deep; over 10 feet of fluid mud and silt with no underwater visibility. The fuselage fragments and the bodies of the two pilots had already been recovered and returned to the Russians but the rest was buried. It was a daunting task but at the end of four weeks we had recovered all that was required. Surprisingly, it was possible to swim through this mud and silt, black and sticky as it was.

The engine needed to be brought out next and this was going to be tense, what with the border between the British and Soviets only about 500 yards downstream from the recovery site. In addition, the physical recovery of the engine was a perilous operation for the divers. The engine, which was three metres long and a metre in diameter had been pulled upright by a crane but remained deep in the mud. The purchase by the crane's grab was very insecure and definitely not suitable for a successful lift which would have to take place at night for added security. One of my corporals managed to fit a steel wire strop to a pipe running along the side of the engine but it was doubtful that this would take the strain.

On the day of the lift, experts arrived from the UK to examine the engine and prepare it for transportation to Britain. Since failure was not an option, I decided to secure the engine as best as possible and I dived down, taking a steel wire strop, and with considerable difficulty passed it right around the engine. I then secured it to itself with a shackle, and tied the loose end to the crane's lifting hook. When darkness fell, with the barge quite crowded with experts, local commanders and the diving team, I dived down again and as the lift began, checked the security of the lifting strops. These tightened as planned and took the immense strain. Worryingly, the crane was operating beyond its designed capacity and as the cables shuddered, they emitted a screaming sound. When I was sure the engine had left the bottom I surfaced and went aboard the barge. I was then asked by one of the experts how many rotor blades the jet had. I thought the question was ridiculous.

"I don't know," I said.

"We do need to know this," the expert said. "If these cables snap, the engine will be lost forever in that mud."

I didn't much fancy the idea of diving beneath the precariously rising engine but down I went, and on reaching the engine felt my way beneath it and counted the rotor blades by touch with the shuddering and whining close to breaking cables above me. Had they snapped that would have been it for me – I would have been buried beneath the massive engine, silt and mud. It was possibly the most dangerous dive of my service career and I resurfaced and made my way onto the barge with a sense of relief. The lift proceeded slowly but surely and eventually the engine lay on the deck of the barge.

The flight Black Box and other pieces of electronic equipment were placed out of sight in an underwater net, secured to the barge and concealed from the Soviet watchers. A few nights later they were surreptitiously loaded into an inflatable dingy. My Corporal and I then swam on the surface towing the dingy to a rendezvous 500 metres downstream towards the Soviet sector. It was a scary task and on reaching the meeting place we were relieved when a few minutes later a Land Rover came across the field to collect it. We then swam back to the barge and returned to barracks.

The whole operation was a strange experience with the diving team taken to and from the site in an enclosed vehicle with blankets over our heads, presumably to prevent us being photographed, identified, and possibly kidnapped. Tensions were high and there were also concerns that the Soviets might send divers underwater to the site. For this reason a small motor boat went up and down the area for most of the day and night randomly dropping small underwater explosive charges as a deterrent. It was odd that only a few weeks earlier we had been working with the Russians to rebuild Skopje.

The recovered engine was dismantled at a research establishment in England then returned to Berlin and onto the barge in neatly labelled pieces, ready to be returned to the Russians. I thought it odd that there was no attempt to conceal the intelligence gathering and when the time came to return the engine, and we moored our barge alongside the Russian's barge and passed the pieces across, the laughing Russians obviously thought the same.

Confined to a secure camp throughout our time in Berlin and flown in and out by the RAF, the so called pleasures of the night life of Berlin were close and yet so far. We had heard that the nightlife was quite racy, especially the Reeperbahn.

As a result of the salvage of the Russian aircraft, I received a Commander-in-Chief BAOR commendation for diving in hazardous conditions.

HEADQUARTERS
BRITISH ARMY OF THE RHINE

24 June 1966

314. Commendation

1. The Commander-in Chief, British Army of the Rhine, wishes to record his appreciation of the conduct displayed by the under-mentioned:

23056357 QMSI S.D. HAMBROOK, RE

2. QMSI Hambrook was a member of a team of Royal Engineer divers from the Advanced Watermanship Training Centre, Kiel, which was employed for a period of three weeks on the salvage of a crashed Russian aircraft. His experience and ability throughout the operation made an important contribution to the success of the salvage works.

3. He dived regularly in very muddy water and soft silt; at one stage his diving was vital in the recovery of one of the aircraft engines which was buried deep in the mud of the lake bottom. To locate the engine he had to feel through four feet of mud at the bottom of an eleven foot hole that had been dug into the lake bottom by a grab. He attached slings to the engine whilst it was still buried in the mud and later attached more slings whilst the engine was lifted by crane above the lake bottom.

4. Conditions for diving were always unpleasant and, during the recovery of the engine, hazardous. He carried out this, the most difficult part of the diving operation, with efficiency and success.

5. The Commander-in Chief directs that an entry be made in the Regimental Conduct Sheet of the above named in accordance with Queen's Regulations para 1633 (o).

Twenty Three

WHEN my time at Kiel drew to a close I received a posting as a Quarter Master Sergeant Instructor to the Joint Services Explosive Ordnance Disposal School. Although a quartermaster is usually one to deal with stores, this posting was a rank between Warrant Officer One and Warrant Officer Two. The school was in Chattenden, Kent on the Isle of Grain and we shared a site with the Royal Engineers' Bomb Disposal Regiment.

Unfortunately, the continual separation caused my wife to seek solace elsewhere and we divorced with shared custody of Stephen and Gareth. She was able to keep the flat. It was sad but she had a new partner and I had to accept the situation. I was philosophical about it. She had been on her own too much of the time.

Chattenden, where I lived on site, was an interesting time with a variety of different experiences. I taught fuze immunisation including how to use liquid nitrogen to disarm battery fuzes by freezing. The battery fuzes, known as the type 50, were designed to be extra sensitive. They had mercury tilt switches which could kill anyone attempting to disarm them. A shift of three degrees would set it off and in addition, it had a ZUS40 anti-extraction device attached. The safest thing to do was to render the batteries inert by freezing them with liquid nitrogen, which we poured in from a cylinder. Nitrogen has a temperature of minus 192 degrees. We tested its condition around the fuze with pieces of cotton wool to see if they froze. Once the ice ring was large enough, we had two hours to move the bombs by putting them on a lorry and taking them to a bomb cemetery to be detonated. The bomb cemetery we used was in Richmond, south-west London and we would have a police escort to ensure our timely arrival.

I also taught chemical and biological weapon disposal and practical demolitions, which was standard NATO training. There were a lot of chemical and biological weapons in service such as nerve agents like mustard gas and VX. It was used during World War One. Mustard gas is a liquid that is fired at the enemy in a shell and on explosion and exposure to the air it turns to gas. One of the tests we ran was to give students a couple of drops of mustard gas on their arm or hand. They had to use the safety swabs they carried and if they didn't do it properly they got a nasty burn.

As part of the chemical training all students and instructors were given gas chamber experience in a sealed Nissen hut. Once inside, with doors closed, the instructor released a canister of gas. I don't remember feeling nervous the first time I did this as I was very experienced and harmful gases were not new to me. The idea was to ensure the students had fitted their suits well. But before leaving the chamber they had to remove their respirators and experience breathing the gas for a short time.

Because I always went into the chamber to ensure the students' safety I found that over time I could endure breathing the gas for longer than any student. An American student challenged me to a gas endurance test so I suggested that we each sang our national anthem knowing full well that The Star Spangled Banner needed deep breaths whereas most of God Save The Queen could be sang whilst exhaling. This coupled with my ability to breathe deeply and hold my breath, thanks to my diving training, ensured that I finished singing while he made a hasty exit.

Until 1970, the chemical protection suit used in disposal operations and training was known as an RAF fuel suit. It was made of thick rubberised material and was difficult to move in. The hood enclosed the head entirely and there was an optical panel. The face mask of a single air cylinder fitted into this and the cylinder was worn on the back, under the suit, with the hood secured around the face mask. In effect the wearer was sealed inside the suit.

When dealing with a chemical or biological incident a line is denoted with a piece of white tape, across which one must be suitably protected by wearing the fuel suit and breathing from the air cylinder. This seems adequate but if the wearer breathes deeply he might use up his air supply. A Swedish air breathing set came onto the market which was far superior to the one in use and I went to the UK agent to assess it for disposal work. It was lighter, slimmer and had a higher capacity, and importantly the air cylinder could be turned on with the air flow activated by the wearer taking a deep breath. This meant greater endurance and could be more easily used with a new protective suit that was in the process of being devised. Unfortunately, a request that the equipment be bought for disposal work was refused. After pressure by the unit commander it was agreed that the need could be explained to the purchasing committee at the MoD and I was detailed to do this.

On the agreed day I went to see the committee of civil servants, taking with me a fuel suit, the air cylinder in current use, and a soldier. I dressed the soldier in the fuel suit and, having turned on the air cylinder, asked all to note the time. I then sealed the hood while explaining to the committee what I was doing, asked the soldier to stand behind me and began to make the case for the new equipment, showing a sample I had borrowed from the agent. While I was doing this there came a disturbance from behind me and I turned to see, as did everyone, the soldier gasping for air and trying to pull off the sealed hood. I released the hood and asked all to note the time. I then explained that the wearer would have had little time to work and that possibly his life would be lost. If a picture is worth a thousand words, so is a practical demonstration. Authorisation was given to purchase the Swedish equipment.

The scientists at the Porton Down chemical warfare centre had devised a protective suit that was easy to put on and take off and was flexible and easy to work in. This went on general issue to the forces and was welcomed in the disposal fraternity as it meant that the wearer had full protection and could move easily. It also made the decontamination process simpler as it was a wear once suit. We wore this with the Swedish breathing equipment.

The students at Chattenden were from all three UK services and included some students from outside NATO such as Iran. On one course we had 10 Persian officers but when the Shah was overthrown they all left immediately, despite the danger to themselves. Very possibly, being officer class, they were some of those slaughtered in their hundreds by the new regime.

All the instructors got on very well and each day we gathered in the crew room for a morning break. Every day one of the American instructors would produce a banana and peel it in the same slow and deliberate manner. One morning I got to his banana before the break and, using an opened paper clip inserted through the side seam, I sliced it into about six slices before putting it back in his lunch box. At the break he produced his banana, peeled it and to his astonishment realised that it was sliced.

Keeping a straight face I said, "Your wife obviously shops at Sainsbury's."

"Yes. How did you know that?"

"Only Sainsbury's sell sliced bananas."

Among the training areas we used was the island of Ordford Ness which was reached by ferry from Ordford village in Suffolk. It was the site of the first nuclear test facility and was out of bounds to most people. We camped there and got on with practising low order detonation techniques on live bombs. Some of these we took to the island, others had been dropped by the Royal Air Force when the island was a bombing range. The island had many deserted but substantial buildings from its nuclear research days, which we were able to camp in.

During my time at the school I passed my Bomb Disposal Engineer Class One exam. I then had two first class trades as well as a qualification as a Fleet Clearance Diver. I strove to maintain the level of fitness acquired at Kiel with daily runs. I enjoyed going out on my own so that I could go as fast as I liked, but also to clear my head.

Twenty Four

ATTACHED to the school was a naval diving team that operated from a depot on the River Medway. Among others duties we supervised continuing training for experienced divers. This included two weeks deep diving at Oban in Scotland. I was paired with an American diver as none of the naval divers seemed to want to dive with him. We enjoyed each other's company above, as well as below, the water. The Commanding Officer of the school at the time was a Lieutenant Commander Royal Navy who wrote in my annual assessment, "A bloody good sailor spoilt by the colour of his uniform." Quite a compliment!

I attended a two-week instructional technique course at HMS *Excellent*, a shore-based establishment in Portsmouth. It was a large building and inside was majestic sweeping steps up to the first floor to the lecture rooms. The right hand stairs were for officers and the left for other ranks, so we parted at the bottom and met at the top. I lived in the mess where the dining room, bar and accommodation rooms were. The waiters were serving sailors and one day I ordered creamed mince on toast for breakfast. It was a popular choice for its high energy, only to have my appetite briefly spoiled when the waiter turned toward the service hatch and called out, "One shit on a raft," which was the nickname of this particular dish. I got on with it.

We learned how to read statistics especially as the lecturer started by saying that 100 per cent of the Wrens in the station were pregnant. Having enjoyed the astonished gasps of everyone in the room he went on to say that there was only one Wren.

"That's why you must not accept statistics but query them." A very valuable lesson.

The navy had generous personal allocations of duty-free tobacco, cigarettes and spirits which they could easily sell when "ashore" and these goods were frequently taken out of the dockyard for this purpose. This was a punishable offence so quite often the dockyard gates would have a search team of Ministry of Defence police there to catch offenders. This difficulty was overcome by the naval gate guard hoisting a "Storm in the Channel" signal, which was three black balls, to warn their comrades of the danger. The MoD police had no idea about signals of course.

The unit diving team kept their skills updated by diving in the wet locks in Chatham Dockyard. One day we were asked to survey the hull of a nuclear submarine that was docked there. The hull of a submarine is immense and few people realise that to reach its deepest parts means a dive down of more than 30 feet. In addition, the gap between the submarine's hull and the side of the lock was narrow and fairly daunting. Having got about halfway down, I heard a very loud clang and I was engulfed in a powerful stream of warm water, possibly from a cooling system. A port about three feet across and six inches thick had been opened and I was extremely lucky that the hatch had not hit me because it would probably have killed me.

Back on the surface I demanded to see the Captain. He had asked for the inspection so he should have known that when divers are alongside you do not open the hatches. He was apologetic.

Once, when training Territorial Army volunteers in bomb disposal techniques, I was approached by a fairly senior officer who was visiting the training sites. He chatted to the men and then to me, asking, "Have you ever been blown up?"

Keeping a straight face, I replied, "No, Sir. I was born looking like this."

While at the school I met Angela. She was the sister of one of the Royal Engineers and came along to a function. We gelled instantly. She had lost her husband to illness and had three young children. We married and were allocated a married quarter fairly close to the school. My boys were still in Brighton and I was able to see them regularly to take them out. Later they were able to come and visit me.

When my tenure at the school was complete after two and a half years, I was posted to 49 Bomb Disposal Squadron Royal Engineers. I moved to a new office 100 yards away and was promoted to Sergeant Major. This meant I was once again actively involved in disposal work and able to put my experience to good use. I was also responsible for discipline among the 180 Royal Engineer soldiers of differing ranks. In the two and a half years that I held that post I only had to charge a Sapper under the disciplinary code once. Most other misdemeanours were dealt with during a walk around the bomb dump and a verbal rollicking. A somewhat backhanded compliment was paid to me was when, at a social event, a sergeant described me to my wife as, "A hard bastard but a fair one."

Twenty Five

ANOTHER interesting incident that occurred was at Petworth in Sussex. A paragraph of about 30 words in a local paper dated August 10, 1969 told of the discovery and making safe of a 250kg German bomb. The biggest part of the story was that local anglers who had been moved to ensure their safety were inconvenienced. Behind this inconvenience lay a task that started with the knowledge that making the bomb safe would involve a wide range of techniques, some of which had not been used for 11 years. No one foresaw the drama of the ending.

In the spring of 1941 a line of bombs fell across the marshy farmland of Rotherbridge Farm near Petworth. Three exploded killing a number of cattle and the fourth left a hole about 20 inches in diameter. No one knew how deep it had gone. The police reported the incident to the Bomb Disposal Unit and a team came out. In the early days of bomb disposal, specialist equipment was at a premium and reserved for bombs whose removal was essential to the war effort or public safety. The Petworth bomb, due to its geographical position ,was unlikely ever to be placed in this category so, after working for several days and encountering considerable difficulty with water and the type of ground, the team was withdrawn and the position of the bomb noted and recorded as abandoned.

Twenty eight years later, the Royal Engineers' Bomb Disposal Unit received a telephone call. The land was due to be developed and the caller was disturbed by a local rumour that an unexploded bomb lay in the area. I came to have a look and it was obvious that the 1941 record was neither accurate nor complete. On top of that, the land above the bomb, wherever it was, was covered in almost three decades of shrubbery.

Two days of patient and diligent detective work followed. We found a shallow depression which had thistles growing on it. There were no thistles anywhere else in the field so this meant that deep earth had probably been disturbed pushing the thistle seeds to the surface. Based on a mixture of calculated assumption and experience, a position was decided upon where the UXB might lay, if it existed at all.

Some days later a location team went to the marked area and, as is procedure, drilled a triangle of holes down 25 feet. The ERA gave positive readings on the second hole but the third could not be drilled deeper than 15 feet due to the presence of a large hard object. The centre of the bomb was determined to be 16 feet 6 inches below the ground. The time that we had spent determining the bomb's position was well spent as it was only two feet from the calculated position. Was it clairvoyance? No, just a mixture of experience, assumption and a feeling in the bones developed over 10 years spent finding and clearing unexploded bombs.

The condition of the marshy ground couldn't have been more difficult. A dewatering plant arrived and, with our help, the operator installed specialised pumping equipment – the excess water taken via a hose into a nearby river. This was essential to pre-drain the area before excavation started. Once installed, this equipment, aided by ancillary pumping sets, was to run for 240 hours, or 10 days, without stopping and would pump over a half a million gallons from the excavation. The land dried out and became more stable and by Monday, August 4, all preparations, including the laying of the template – part of the pre-fabricated timber set for us to work inside – was complete.

I then took command of the operation. All excavation was to be by hand as the unstable strata could not be mechanically excavated. The trench would be fitted with shafting timbers to prevent the hole from caving in. There was still a little water flowing in, bringing fines from the soil with it and this was to be observed. I had planned for the men to work two shifts of seven hours per shift. However, as no accommodation could be found where the landladies would agree to provide meals at a very early or a very late hour, the working day would start at 7am and run until 6pm. The engineers, plant operators and fitters were on site working 24 hours on, 24 hours off, tending to the dewatering and power equipment.

Excavations started in earnest on August 4, a Tuesday, and proceeded with little difficulty through clay, gravel and fluid sand until 11.25am on the Saturday when a battered and crumpled tail unit was recovered at a depth of 13 feet 3 inches. This was positively identified as a tail unit from a 250kg bomb, a bomb fitted with an extremely sensitive and excitable clockwork fuze. This was prone to restarting if subjected to even a slight degree of vibration. Headquarters were told and requested to load the immunisation and make-safe equipments and dispatch them to the site.

The shaft had been excavated down 14 feet through the unstable and changing strata layers into hard, dark blue clay in which the bomb lay. The blue clay lay on running sand through which flowed a multitude of underground streams, which gushed up into the shaft through breaks in the clay floor bringing sand fines and forming a rising bottom. The only way to counter this, and to prevent losing the bomb, was to excavate more than flowed into the shaft and to work without stopping until the bomb was uncovered and made safe.

Following a quick reorganisation of labour, a briefing of everyone on site as to the urgency and method of work and a warning that I, as Squadron Sergeant Major, was about to change from my normal happy self into a rear-kicking, snarling slave driver until the bomb was uncovered, and with a cry of, "Let's shift muck," the chase was on. A further three feet was excavated. The rising bottom was kept down by plugging the shaft bottom with a layer of sandbags and the water kept down by another continually running pumping set. By 5pm the bomb lay uncovered. It was in mint condition and so well preserved by the blue clay that the paint and stencil markings on the casing were intact and legible. The fuze head was cleaned and immediately identified as a 17 series much to be respected clockwork fuze. This is one which presents a very real threat to bomb disposers even after 20 years buried in the earth. During the cleaning of the bomb casing around the fuze pocket, a slight weeping of a dark oily liquid smelling strongly of ammonia, recognised as being nitro glycerine, was seen coming from the fuze pocket weld.

A plan, prearranged with the local police, to clear and seal the area to all but the disposal team was put into operation, and by 6pm the area was quiet. There weren't many houses nearby anyway. The only sound was the thudding of the pump, a sound so familiar with the disposal team that it was almost unnoticeable. At 6.30pm, after having been previously alerted, the Troop Commander Captain English arrived at the site bringing with him the required immunisation equipment. He checked that the enforced precautions were adequate and conferred with me. After a further inspection of the bomb it was decided to enforce evacuation from the site of everyone except English and I until the fuze had been immunised, the source of nitro glycerine leakage established and the main filling identified. After preparing the equipment, Captain English and I descended into the 17 foot deep shaft that resounded to the continuous roar and vibration of the pumping equipment. This could not be stopped if immediate flooding, and possible collapse of the shaft, were to be avoided. It was decided that the use of the electronic stethoscope, designed to give warning of a fuze being reactivated, was demoralising because we couldn't hear it due to the pumps. It would be impossible to pick out the light ticking of a clock from the bedlam issuing from the headphones. Doing the only thing possible we ignored the fact that the fuze, in an excellent condition, may have been ticking and could explode the bomb at any moment. Captain English and I continued to ignore this for a further 10 hours.

The fuze was drilled prior to immunisation. One man drilled and the other kept a steady but gentle flow of water around the drill to keep the trickle of nitro glycerine from being detonated by the warming drill point.

With the hole drilled the equipment was quickly connected into the fuze and 30 minutes later, with the immunisation complete, we came up for a break and, at a safe distance from the shaft, the remainder of the team were briefed and all but five were stood down until the next day at 9am.

At 8pm the work restarted, this time to gain access to the main filling of the bomb for identification prior to removal. As the bomb was in excellent condition and not rusty, it was decided to remove the base plate by unscrewing it, rather than cut a hole in the bomb casing, and this proved almost as easily done as said, the base plate being only a little more than hand tight. As this was unscrewed and removed from the bomb, the pit quickly became filled with extremely strong, bitter, acrid fumes, emanating from the bomb's interior, similar to old fashioned smelling salts.

It caused us to cough, retch and feel nauseous until the task was completed nine hours later. Inspection of the bomb filling showed it to have been powder filled and that the filling had deteriorated to such an extent that some two gallons of nitro glycerine – the most concentrated unstable and catastrophic explosive of all – had been formed as a product of deterioration. This now lay in the bomb with the remaining 200lbs of hardened powder explosive either floating as lumps in the nitro glycerine or adhering to the bomb casing. No tools or specialised techniques exist for such a situation and the only solution was removal by hand. Two wooden spatulas were made in hopes we could scoop out the nitro glycerine using these, but this wasn't feasible.

Strict instructions were given that no one was to approach within 200 yards of the shaft during the removal of the filling. To enable us to reach freely into the bomb, without snagging, and to minimize the risk of friction causing a detonation, we removed all clothing above the waist and took it in turns to reach through the base aperture and gently sieve through the nitro glycerine for the lumps of powder. These then had to be broken between the fingers before being withdrawn from the bomb and placed into water soaked sandbags for removal and disposal. The liquid nitro glycerine was placed into sawdust filled buckets for later disposal by burning. A sergeant was positioned at the top of the shaft to watch for signs that we might be overcome by fumes. The sergeant remained in this position acting as safety and contact man for some eight hours without rest.

Putting your hand into nitro glycerine can be likened to putting it into ice cold slush. It stings and is very painful on any skin break and around the fingernails. Unless one is completely devoid of human responses this requires, at the least, a stiff upper lip! It was not possible to wear gloves because of the danger of them filling with nitro glycerine which would then have been solidified by the warmth of the hands, making their removal problematic.

The spotlights attracted myriads of insects, among them vicious mosquitoes that took immediate advantage of our rain soaked semi naked bodies and had the feed of a lifetime. By this time we were both feeling utterly frustrated. The natural reaction to a bite is to slap the insect quick and hard, but with hands and arms encrusted with nitro glycerine a slap could have developed into a bang, so we had to ignore the bites. We couldn't chat as we worked as that would have meant us taking in more breath than necessary and breathing equipment would have been too cumbersome.

The work of extracting the explosive progressed slowly. We changed jobs frequently – one reaching into the bomb and the other bagging explosive, diluting nitro glycerine and trying to minimize the risk of explosion by washing down the bomb case and working area. Finally at 5am on Sunday the bomb was sufficiently clean of explosive to enable the fuze pocket to be cut out of the bomb for removal from the shaft and the fuze pocket was then detonated to remove the danger of the uncertain fuze.

All uncertainty removed, it was now time to relax, and we both settled down to a quiet cup of tea and a smoke. I had worked for 29 hours without warm food or rest. I had lost most of the skin from the soles of both feet due to them being saturated for most of the time. Both of us had been exposed to extreme danger from the uncertain fuze and a very unstable explosive for 11 hours without a break. We just did, without hesitation, what we thought had to be done in a normal bomb disposal operation. It may appear that the task revolved around two men, but this was not so, and both of us, if asked, would say that the successful completion of the task and disposal of the bomb was a result of the careful planning, preparation, support and hard work of the Bomb Disposal Unit, RE.

Having disposed of the bomb, all that remained to be done was the refilling of the shaft (1,224 cubic feet of earth excavated by hand in four days) and the withdrawal of all plant and equipment to the Unit HQ at Chattenden. This took a further four days of hard labour until finally the site was returned to the owners with little to show that a bomb had ever been there other than that small paragraph in the local newspaper bemoaning the fact that the local anglers had been inconvenienced. One of the lads had gone to buy some cigarettes from a shop and came back with the local newspaper. It made me laugh.

Twenty Six

M Y NEXT job was a deployment to the Shetland Islands to clear a former Commando training area, Sullom Voe, ready for development. I flew to Aberdeen and arranged for the men, vehicles and stores to arrive via the Aberdeen Steam Ship company. I was booked into the Lerwick Hotel. It was old but comfortable and had obviously been recently refurbished. My toilet was in a fairly large room that might have been a single bedroom before being converted. The toilet pan itself was fitted almost in the centre of the room, perhaps by a plumber with a sense of humour, since the toilet roll holder was screwed to a wall well out of reach when sat on the pan.

On arrival I borrowed a vehicle and drove out to Sullom Voe to gauge the mission ahead. Sullom Voe was a peninsula that also spread inland by about half a mile. The ground was undulating and very rough and I estimated that a surface sweep would take six to eight weeks. I visited the island GP to book the team into the surgery in case we needed medical cover and while chatting to him I learned that any laundry we had would have to be shipped to Aberdeen, laundered and the shipped back again. I remarked that anyone setting up a launderette would make a fortune.

When the men and vehicles arrived after a long and torturous three day drive, we quickly sorted the equipment ready to start. Everything had arrived except the service explosives container which was not allowed onto the ferry and was placed in a secure store to be collected on our return. The steam company informed me that if we needed explosive I could buy commercial explosives from the company itself. The shipping companies up there seemed to supply everything.

The following day we deployed to the site and having briefed the men and divided them into search teams the surface sweep started. The weather was reasonable and good progress was made. After a week, about a quarter of the sweep had been completed and no dangerous items were found. In the evenings we mixed with the locals and the cosmopolitan crowd of merchant seamen who used the Shetlands as a stopover. They included Russians and other nationalities, all of whom readily socialised. We were invited to a wedding. The celebrations went on for a whole weekend and well into the Monday. There was a lot of drinking and when stocks ran low the host offered items from his home for sale to raise money to buy more. I bought a sheepskin rug for £5 but some days later, when the groom was sober, I gave it back to him. I did wonder what the bride remembered of her wedding night.

After a month the area had been thoroughly searched and nothing dangerous found. It was declared safe. I did wonder what sort of development would take place in such a remote area. We left the Shetlands and took the ferry back to Aberdeen with our vehicles and equipment. Once there I retrieved the stored explosives and we started the three day road journey back to the unit. When we got back, everyone went on a week's leave except me as I had five weeks of work to catch up on. I later learned that the Sullom Voe oil and gas storage was being constructed on the site we'd proved safe and that the doctor had financed and opened a launderette. I am sure he made the fortune that I predicted.

Twenty Seven

MY DIVING skills were constantly useful to me, including during an incident in Leamington Spa. A local sub-aqua diver thought he saw a bomb on the river bed and reported it to the police. The unit diving team and I deployed to investigate and, after 45 minutes of searching the muddy bottom in low visibility, I found an RAF 25lb practise bomb, and brought it ashore. These bombs have a small explosive and flash charge in them. They activate on impact so that the accuracy of the drop can be observed. The safest means of disposing of them is by using a small explosive charge to split them open which also causes the contents to ignite. We transported the bomb to a nearby field to do this.

Another unusual incident followed when a former soldier reported what he thought was an exposed mine in Mote Park near Maidstone, Kent. It was a popular park with play areas, lake and natural woodland and the Home Guard had been using it as a training area.

A site visit confirmed that the soldier was right – it was a Mark 5 anti-tank mine which could be easily disarmed. Having done so, and removed the mine, we returned to the site some days later to carry out a precautionary sweep using mine detectors. We recovered another 10 Mark 5 anti-tank mines all of which were fuzed. Presumably the Home Guard had laid them and forgotten them when they disbanded as the war ended. This was fairly common. A housing estate at Rowner near Portsmouth was built over such a mine training area and there were a number of other such incidents.

UXBs can be discovered by sight and by detectors, but I also had another means at my disposal since I have an ability to locate buried items using divining rods made from metallic welding rods. This was something I had taken an interest in as a young man, probably from books I bought or borrowed from the library. I used welding rods as the ones recommended in the book were very expensive.

They work like this – you hold the rods at chest height, parallel to the ground and think a thought, such as *I am sitting in a rocking chair*. If you are indeed in a rocking chair, the rods will vibrate and move slowly towards each other. If you are sitting in a different kind of chair, or not sitting at all, then the rods will stay still. It works. I don't know how, but it does. It works better when you are tired, perhaps because your mind is clearer?

One of the tasks I used the rods for was the location of live and dead underground electric cables that had been laid in a training camp area near Durham. The area consisted of concrete slabs ready to have tents erected on them with a mix of new and old power connections to each. The area was to be developed by the holding unit but the danger from the live cables and obstruction caused by the defunct ones was considered such that our unit was tasked to locate and mark their positions.

Using mine detecting equipment is not always possible where live cables might interfere. I have always believed that the majority of people have the ability to carry out simple divining, provided they are convinced that it works and believe they can do it. I arrived on site with a bundle of welding rods and explained to the 20-strong working party what they needed to do, then gave a practical demonstration. I had the first 10 men trying it out over the concrete slabs whilst thinking, *Concrete slabs*. To their astonishment when they did this, the rods moved in on themselves but when they thought of a different material, they straightened. The second group of 10 men were not quite so successful with only eight of them showing the ability.

Those that could divine were paired off and two divining pairs worked up to and around the slabs in turn with one pair thinking, *Live cable*, and the second thinking, *Dead cable*. They had wooden pegs with which to mark what they found and quite soon there were marking pegs, inserted in lines marking the underground cables. My Sappers were proud of their achievements but the site commander expressed doubts over the accuracy until he was invited to try for himself and found that he could do it too.

"Life is full of surprises," I said to him.

We remained on site for some weeks until it was agreed that all cables, live or not, had been located and their position marked with the surface pegs.

I was also able to use a pendulum to find things on a drawing or map. During the war, the Japanese occupied Malay and stored their bombs and munitions in four tunnels drilled into a mountain at Penang. As time went on, all but one of the entrances collapsed and there was no specific information as to where they were. The unit who were tasked to clear the area of munitions worked through the open tunnel and all the explosive items they found were put onto a landing craft, taken out to sea and dumped in deep water. Using a large scale map of the immediate area and my pendulum I was able to locate the approximate entrances to the other three tunnels which were also cleared.

I enjoyed research on such matters and, similarly, was always keen to research all I could about bombs. Whenever I was defusing a difficult bomb, I would look up and read the latest intelligence on it. For example, during the Second World War when the Germans realised that we were defusing their bombs safely, they began adding new fuzes. I was amazed to hear that the German bomb makers had patented a lot of their fuzes, the plans for which were lodged in the patents office in London; although I've no proof of that.

Twenty Eight

IN THE early stages of the Second World War many airfields and strategic crossroads were mined in anticipation of an invasion. The mines were made from standard water piping of three to six inches in diameter screwed together to make lengths of up to 60 feet. These were forced into the ground at an angle so that the far end would be about eight feet deep. They were filled with commercial Polar Dynamite and linked to a firing circuit with the aim of forming craters. These would prevent aircraft landing or free movement by vehicles. Thankfully their use was not necessary as Britain was not invaded, but they did need to be removed, not least because the explosive filling would deteriorate and become dangerous. The removal was done with hand powered pneumatic extractors. These sometimes caused part of the pipe to break, leaving an explosive length somewhere underground and often abandoned. The mine was then marked as cleared.

The difficulty of clearing these and making them safe was that they had been laid hastily during the Phony War by British and Canadian troops who were possibly not engineers and therefore did not appreciate the importance of accurate records. As a result, there were some fatalities.

The unit had one back actor digger – a tractor with an earth grab – that could be operated by remote control, giving the operator and excavation team some safety. We used this at Ford, a former RAF fighter airfield, where we were clearing these sorts of mines but as more heavily mined sites required fairly urgent clearance, in the short term these mines were uncovered by hand. This was extremely dangerous.

I was sent to appear at St Christopher House, before a Ministry of Defence committee who were responsible for supplying the engineers with equipment, including remote control plants. As I was explaining the danger and urgency, the meeting was interrupted by a telephone call from my unit. The back actor at Ford had been badly damaged by an exploding mine. This added weight to my submissions and the purchase of another six machines was authorised, but not before I was asked if I had arranged for this to happen.

In 1969, excavation work during the construction of the M23 near Fleet in Hampshire was stopped when a 500kg unexploded bomb was found. It took the Troop Commander and I an hour to get there and when we did we found that the bomb was completely exposed. It had two fuze pockets, one containing a 17-clockwork fuze and the other the dreaded 50 battery anti-handling fuze. A microphone was placed on the bomb and no ticking could be heard. A message was passed to HQ requesting follow up equipment and while we waited for this, we drilled the clockwork fuze and injected a clock stopping fluid into it. This was initially salt water, and later became a gel. We left the 50 Series fuze alone.

When the follow up equipment and men arrived the magnetic clock stopper was readied as a backup, the steam generator and air compressor prepared for use, and the trepanner made ready. It was going to be a long night.

Having briefed the men we positioned the trepanner and moved to a safe place while the bomb casing was trepanned. This took just over 30 minutes. When the grinding tone stopped we knew that the bomb casing had been cut through and that we had a hole, three inches in diameter, through which we could identify the filling.

The trepanner was removed and the steam hose feeder fitted and started, melting the filling, which we would then remove. It took until 10am the following morning to do this. When the bomb was empty it was cooled with water then explosive charges were placed inside on the two fuze pockets and simultaneously detonated but not before we warned the police and cleared the site of men. I detonated the charges remotely, checked we had been successful, then the site was cleared of safety cordon, vehicles and equipment and we returned to our barracks.

I was in touch with my parents regularly, but I wasn't able to tell them about my work. It would have been detrimental to public confidence if people knew exactly how much unexploded ordnance was lying about all over the country. Anyone assumed that after the war ended, everything was safe and the government wasn't going to tell people different.

Twenty Nine

I N OCTOBER 1969, during excavation work at Chalk Farm in Camden, London, a plant operator uncovered what appeared to him to be the side of a metallic globe, possibly made of aluminium, in the side of a trench about eight foot deep. He immediately stopped work, the find was reported to the police, and our unit was contacted. The duty officer and myself left the barracks and met a police escort who could get us through the midday traffic and quickly to the site.

Initially it seemed that the item might be an aircraft's external oxygen cylinder. But a few minutes of gentle digging exposed a screw-fastened plate and, due to my training with the navy, I realised that this was the nose of an anti-shipping mine – often used as a parachute mine. We could see four inches of a cylindrical mine, which was 10 feet long and contained a variety of firing devices, as well as 1500lbs of high explosive. It was the first mine of this type to be found on land in more than 25 years.

The situation was complicated. The area was densely occupied with a secondary school just 200 yards away. Main tube train lines ran underground quite close to us. The reason these mines were used was because when they exploded they caused complete destruction of structures within a radius of 440 yards and damage over a much wider area. They were very effective blast bombs.

Whilst our HQ was alerted to the nature of the UXB, we discussed evacuation, traffic diversions and stopping the tubes with the police. It was decided that the task, apart from the microphone listening watch which was put in place immediately, would be delayed until 6pm that evening.

When the time came, the site fell quiet. A local community centre provided overnight accommodation for residents who had no family to go to and the Red Cross opened its kitchen to cater for them.

The mine was buried at a right angle to the trench wall, parallel to the surface. We faced about 24 hours of very dangerous digging to reach the fuze pockets. A simpler solution was to remove the exposed filling plate which was about six inches in diameter and steam the explosive out that way.

The steamer was made ready, the hoses run out and with the plate off, I gently chiselled at the face of the cast explosive to form a cavity for the steam to work more efficiently. There was no steam hose feeder which could be used as this was such an unusual find. Instead, we fed the hose manually into the mine and as the effluence containing the melted explosive needed to be periodically collected I decided that it was my responsibility to stay at the mine and call forward help to collect the effluence as necessary.

The press seemed to be everywhere and I convinced my officer that he should deal with this and keep them off the site. At some point during the night, though, I heard voices and looked up to see a gaggle of reporters and photographers at one end of the trench. I was more than annoyed and told them in no uncertain terms that they were exposing themselves and me to extreme danger, and they left.

During the night there was a loud bang, the steamer had seemingly ruptured a fuel pipe and caught fire. The support party moved the vehicles away from the danger and put out the fire. Once inspected it was realised that the pipe had not ruptured but come loose and the support party worked quickly to rejoin it. When steaming out is interrupted a very real danger arises that potentially a vacuum will be formed by the stoppage of steam, drawing explosive into the pipe and causing the face of the steamed explosive to become highly sensitive to heat. After about 20 minutes the steamer was again active and the process restarted with low pressure steam to clear the sensitive face. A short time later the pressure was increased and once again molten explosive started to flow.

Later in the night when there were two of us at the mine, a section of the trench wall above the mine gave way and started to slide down but I was able to get my arms around it and push it away to one side and let it fall to the floor. And so the night went on until at about 7am the mine was clear of explosives. The effluence residue was taken and over 25 bags of resolidified explosive was loaded onto a truck and despatched with a police escort to our HQ, from where it was taken to a demolition ground for disposal by controlled burning.

Explosive charges were made up and using a length of flat wood, we reached into the mine and placed them on the exploder pockets. At an arranged time I lit the fuze to the charges and retired to join the section in a safe area. Having heard the charge and fuze pockets detonate, and with the remnants inspected to ensure nothing dangerous remained, the site was declared safe and all restrictions lifted just in time for the morning rush hour, for the tube trains to start running and for the school to open. All the equipment was loaded for the return to camp, the men were gathered and thanked for their efforts and support through the night and sent back to camp. We thanked the police and then various council representatives arrived. After answering their questions, I returned to camp with the luxury of a blue light police escort out of London.

Before we left, a journalist had some questions for us and seemed to want to say that it was all my work.

"No," I said. "This is a crew. A bloody good crew."

He ran the story and A Bloody Good Crew was the headline.

Bomb disposal is the most dangerous job in the military, and you have to look after your men and yourself. Without thinking about it deeply, I developed a little phrase I would say, "Home, bath and bed." It became my way of closing the door on the day's events – signing off physically and mentally. Then, when I went home I would chat to my wife, never about work but other things that could take my mind off it. It was my way of debriefing.

I was curious about the mine. It was inexplicable that it should be there and buried so deeply. So, some days later, I returned to Camden and went to the council office to examine the wartime ARP records. I found that one morning in 1941 a mine parachute was found dangling from the roof on the corner of a nearby block of flats which overlooked where the mine was discovered. From this I deduced that nearing earth the parachute snagged the roof and became detached from the mine, which had swung out, over and into the ground where it was found some 28 years later. The residents of the block of flats and many other homes had a very lucky escape that night in 1941. I received a letter from a little girl who lived there and I wrote back. We kept in touch for 30 years in the end, sharing our lives and what was going on. She moved to America but came to back to England several times.

Some weeks later I received a letter from Camden Town Council asking if I had any objection to having one of the accommodation blocks being built named as Hambrook Court. I regarded this as an honour. My wife and I were invited to the naming ceremony and had an enjoyable day in Camden. Three years ago my daughter Daniell took my granddaughter Tara to see, "Granddad Steve's flats." A man stopped them to ask if they were lost and when she explained what they were doing, he said that it was his brother who had been excavating and who had discovered the bomb.

Thirty

AFTER Chalk Farm we were called to one of the Walthamstow reservoirs in east London. It was being drained for maintenance work when a suspicious object was seen. I identified an unexploded parachute mine. Not one for 25 years and now two in six weeks! Access to the area was difficult as there was a muddy shallow creek which our vehicles could not cross. The police were informed and left to safeguard the site while I returned to HQ. It was decided that a simple floating bridge would be used. This, with the weight of the truck on it, would sink into the mud and provide a stable crossing for the equipment carrying and towing vehicles. We began at 5am the following morning, the convoy of vehicles arrived, and the bridge made. By late afternoon, everything was ready for the disposal process.

It was decided that the safest and easiest means of disposal would be that that was used on the Camden mine but first the mine was rolled onto a plastic sheet and wrapped to insulate it from the cold mud and retain the steam heat. It would have taken a lot more heat to melt the explosive otherwise and it's best to keep the process as short as possible. But even then it took all night.

My Commanding Officer and I did the rolling, having moved the men back for their safety. Once this was done the filling plate was removed and the steam generator and steam hoses readied for use. At this time a Royal Navy clearance team arrived. Although the prime responsibility was theirs they did not possess the equipment to deal with it as planned so it became a joint operation. I think they were niggled about the publicity we'd had for the bomb at Chalk Farm, which was one of the reasons they turned up. Their commander was an officer who I knew well from various diving experiences. I wore my diving suit throughout the operation.

The steaming started slowly as the steam hoses had to run over about 100 yards of very cold mud. The steam pressure at the mine was fairly low but with time it built up although it did mean that the operation was going more slowly than normal and would last well into, or even overnight. The constant feeding of the steam nozzle into the mine and collection of the explosive effluence went on throughout the early hours until only the casing and fuze exploder pockets remained to be cooled before being detonated.

At about 10am the following day, after the police cordon had been warned, the charges were prepared, placed into the mine and fired remotely. As the mine was on the surface its fragments were widely dispersed and a site search was made to ensure nothing dangerous was left of it. During this search one of the naval team came to me carrying an intact exploder pocket with fuze. I could see that the fuze head had sheared off and the time seal appeared loose with only a few seconds left to run. I quietly told him to stand still, called for the other searchers to move away, got him to gently pass it to me and then move away. I then carefully placed it on the ground where it was later explosively destroyed but not before I told the sailor of his gross stupidity, which was even more remarkable since he was a trained clearance diver. He had endangered himself and all on site.

Another site search was carried out and all being clear we began to get the vehicles and equipment back over the creek, and recovered the timbers we used to bridge it. Having been on site for more than 24 hours, we thanked the police and returned to camp.

The beginning. First bomb disposal course at Broadbridge Heath, 1954. Second from the left in the top row.

Sweeping for B type C anti-tank mines on Littlehampton beach, 1956. Three million were laid on Britain's coastal areas.

Locating UXBs at Winfrith Heath, decoy area for Southampton.

Bomb Disposal Troop Sergeant, Malta Fortress Squadron Royal Engineers.

Floriana, Malta.

The Rotunda of Mosta, Malta.

Malta Fortress Squadron Royal Engineers.

Rabat, Malta where a donkey had a very narrow escape.

Bailey bridge built by Royal Engineers in an attempt to rescue workers at the Ta' Qali reservoir collapse in Malta.

Constructing two camps and four schools at Skopje in the former Yugoslavia, after an earthquake left 200,000 people without homes.

Winter diving in Kiel, northern Germany.

Diving the River Havel, Berlin to recover a Soviet fighter jet. This was the most dangerous dive of my career.

A dose of CS gas when instructing at Joint Services Explosive Ordnance Disposal School, Chattenden.

1969. Working through the night after the construction of the M23 near Fleet in Hampshire reveals a 500kg bomb.

The M23 bomb, a combination of clockwork and battery fuzes designed to kill bomb disposal personnel.

A press photo for George Fletcher and myself. We are pictured with a landmine similar to that which we defused at Chalk Farm.

Smiling with relief after defusing a 250kg bomb on a farm in Reading.

Named as the army's Man Of The Year, 1970. Not long after I received the George Medal for gallantry from HM The Queen.

Hong Kong, instructing Ghurka Sappers in diving.

Enjoying a barbecue in Hong Kong. This was a thank you from the Ghurkas we were instructing.

Selected for commission, on September 25, 1973, I became Lieutenant Hambrook RE GM

Remembrance Day at the Allied War Memorial on the outskirts of Kiel, northern Germany.

1982, The Falklands.

Cruising the Mississippi River in 1982.

The Falklands. Commanding clearance, defusing a 1,000 pound bomb – a live weapon, another of which had already killed a colleague.

Extracted by hand on Stanley Airfield.

My BLESMA award (1987) and Zimba the dog.

Meeting HM The Queen at a garden party. I was fortunate enough to attend four of these lovely events.

Remembrance Day, Horseguards Parade.

Remembrance Day. I attended at the Cenotaph for a period spanning 30 years.

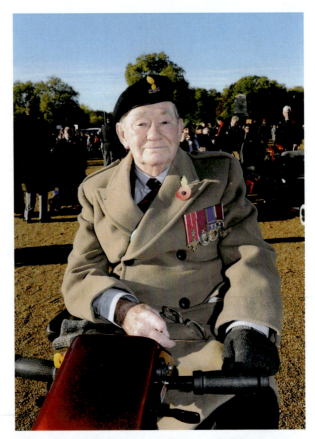

My medals.

Thirty One

I WAS off on my travels again, this time to Sardinia where there was a multinational rocket research facility and range. A surface to surface rocket had failed shortly after launch and it was believed that the warhead had detonated on impact. It needed to be located and some parts recovered. There was competition between the companies working on the facility and the British Aircraft Corporation (BAC,) who was paying the Ministry of Defence for my services.

After attending the medical centre for vaccinations, I was briefed on my flights and issued with a hand held surface locator which folded in on itself into a box. I wore civilian clothing to travel and carried no passport as I was told my NATO pass and service identity card would be sufficient, however, we had a transfer at Rome airport and without my passport, I was apprehended. The Italian police thought the locator was a weapon. After an exchange of telephone calls I was able to join the onward flight to Sardinia.

On arrival I was met by a BAC representative who took me to the range's personnel camp. I was given a sparsely furnished room in which I changed into my working uniform. Having been advised not to drink the local water and that there was an epidemic of hepatitis – against which I was not inoculated – I went to a pharmacy near the camp entrance and bought bottled water and paid for an injection, the second of which would follow two days later. It was the first time had been told to drop my trousers in a crowded shop!

The various company representatives lived in a nearby hotel. Before I started I was taken to the on-site ops room and shown a film of the rocket falling and impacting. It was obvious to me that the warhead had not detonated as thought and what had been seen was only the fuel exploding. When you get a detonation there's a shockwave that I personally think is visible. Maybe it's only visible to someone with a lot of experience. In addition, there was no cracking sound that would have been heard on detonation.

Italy still had National Service and any recruit with a criminal record was enlisted and sent to Sardinia, as were any officers who had blighted their career. It was a difficult working environment especially I was given about 40 soldiers as searchers, none of whom spoke English, and an interpreter who often did not turn up for work. I had use of a battered jeep and a soldier driver.

The area we were due to search was fairly narrow, about 250 yards across, but several miles long – directly under the flight path of the rocket – and an extremely difficult, rough terrain. I split the men into two search parties and if they found something of interest, they called me. We were looking for the arming clock, which armed the whole device and was about the size of an orange. My physical fitness was a great asset to enable me to move between the two groups.

The men were just not used to being treated as I would treat one of my soldiers so I had no choice but to become a shouting bully, which got them working and caused no noticeable resentment. I occasionally had to break up fights which became quite frequent so whilst intervening I carried a spade.

As the search moved into its third week the physical distance between the groups became greater and it became difficult for me to maintain control so I asked my HQ for help and four days later one of my Corporals arrived. Having briefed him on the task and the danger of the local water, and ensured that he had adequate accommodation, he was introduced to the searchers and took control of one of the groups and learnt to be like me in dealing with them. This enabled the searching to proceed faster and after a further two weeks it moved forward into the impact area. Soon, fragments were being found, and near the shallow crater, caused by the missile impacting, there were the remains of the shattered but undetonated warhead from which I was able to extract the arming clock. This was handed to the BAC officer for forensic testing and I stood the searchers down after thanking them for their efforts. I set fire to the remaining explosive.

As a thank you we were taken on a daytrip to the coast which was some distance away. We passed through an area known as the Moon Plain where many impressive rock outcrops gave the impression that we could be on another planet. The seaside town we went to was large and touristy but the amenities were based on European tastes, even down to fish and chips, which detracted from its authenticity. It was like going to Brighton and I would have preferred something different, although I'm sure we made do with a good drink.

At the end of the evening we started the return journey. As we passed through a very isolated village we ran out of fuel. The driver knocked on a nearby door to ask for help and we were all asked to go into the building where the villainous looking owner questioned us about our presence in Sardinia. I felt uncomfortable as the Mafia was very active in Sardinia and even more uncomfortable when several more similarly sinister looking men came into the building. The BAC officer entered into negotiations to obtain fuel and also let it known that we were workers from the rocket range which also employed local residents. This seemed to ease the tension and after some time a can of fuel was sold to us and we left as quickly as we could. Crossing the Moon Plain in the dark was fascinating with the outcrops looming up from the blackness. When we were safely back at the range and chatting over a nightcap it became apparent that the range regulars thought we'd been lucky to escape unscathed as the Mafia are known to kidnap people.

Some days later the Corporal and I were on a flight on our way to the UK. Throughout our stay I had bought medical necessities and bottled water for myself and then both of us, keeping the receipts as I expected to have the expenses refunded. I submitted the usual claim form only to have it rejected as not authorised. Tongue in cheek I wrote on the rejected claim form "authorised by the Senior British Medical Officer Sardinia" signed and resubmitted it. It was paid!

Back in the UK, work went on with little respite. Reports were constant with some of them resulting in a bomb or dangerous ordnance being found, but others being nothing at all. Either way, the public who acted in good faith were thanked.

In February 1970, a farmer in Reading reported an explosion in one his fields. I went to the site and was shown a crater from which I gathered some fragments of an exploded 250kg German bomb. The farmer knew the bomb was there because 30 years previously in 1940, a stick, or line of bombs dropped across his farm. Some exploded but two others did not and he assumed that because of that they were safe and filled in the holes of entry. But now he was worried about the other one and he took me to where he could vaguely remember it being. No surface indication remained but close to the spot he pointed at the only thistle clump in the field – similar to Petworth. I knew that sometimes deep root growth would grow in the disturbed soil so I decided that was the point at which to start the water jetting and location, which we did some days later. Almost immediately we had a positive result which indicated a large metal object at a depth of 19 feet – almost certainly the second bomb. The standard shafting equipment came out from camp and having laid a template, which ensures that the revetting is properly installed, the excavation started. Reading University, a tower block with many windows facing the site, was close enough to be damaged with casualties if things went wrong so the police cordoned off the farm and closed the university for 48 hours.

At 11 feet the crumpled tail unit of a 250kg bomb was recovered which indicated the possible fuzing. The bomb's trace through the subsoil could now be probed using the non-magnetic probe which, using threaded sections, could be extended to 12 feet. Probing down the trace, contact was made with a hard object that we presumed was the bomb, and a microphone watch established. Digging continued until at 18 feet the base of a 250kg bomb was exposed. Careful digging completely uncovered the bomb and the fuze was identified as the clockwork 17 series. The Troop Officer came to the site and as the fuze was inactive it was decided to trepan the bomb and steam out the main filling and then destroy the fuze. During this operation a listening watch was maintained remotely and in the shaft. All went well and after some six hours the bomb was empty and the explosive effluence collected for burning. The fuze and exploder pocket seemed to be loose and a hard pull broke it away from its fractured fixing. It was placed on the shaft floor, sand bagged and remotely detonated, the bomb casing brought to the surface and the cordon and safety measures relaxed. Why the first bomb had exploded was not known although reports had been received from Germany stating that some allied bombs had spontaneously detonated in recent years due to deteriorating explosive and perhaps this was the reason. The farmer should have reported the bombs at the time.

Thirty Two

O N FRIDAY, April 18, 1970 I received a message. I was to report to my Commanding Officer on Monday at 9am. This usually meant that I was going away so I packed a travel bag and off I went. In his office I was handed a sealed envelope.

"Open it," he told me. And when I did, I was astounded to read that I had been awarded the George Medal for my operational work and that the award would be made public the following day. I rang the local school where my wife worked to tell her, then left for Birling Gap near Seaford on the coast of Sussex where a B type C mine had been reported.

The report was correct and having explained to the police that the mine needed to be detonated, I selected a protected area close to the foot of the cliffs. There, once I made up the explosive charge and placed it on the mine, I could retire to it as a safe spot for remote detonation. The blast wave was deflected by the cliff face and as I looked up I saw a section had broken away and was falling toward me! I thought it to be just my luck to gain a decoration and be crushed all in the same day but fortunately it fell some yards away. When speaking to my OC about this he laughed and said that he had passed the callout to me to get me to relax after the excitement of the morning. That evening I rang my mother, brothers and sons to tell them about my award. They were delighted and Mum sent me a congratulatory telegram.

The following day was absolute bedlam as I and the officer who had dealt with the mine at Chalk Farm in Camden Town had been awarded the George Medal; he for that incident and myself for the Petworth and M23 bombs and the land mine. At 9am there was a press call at the unit where many reporters, photographers and television crews asked questions, called for poses and one to one interviews. This lasted for over two hours until we went to our respective messes to receive the congratulations of the mess members and to have a drink. I had arranged for my wife to drive me into camp in the morning and to pick me up after lunch because I knew I'd be over the drink-drive limit by then. It was a confusing day with all the questions coming from a packed press conference of print and television journalists, but a happy day as well.

◈ ◈ ◈

THE LONDON GAZETTE, 21st APRIL 1970
ARMY DEPARTMENT
CENTRAL CHANCERY OF THE ORDERS OF
KNIGHTHOOD

St. James's Palace, London, SW1
21st April 1970

The QUEEN has been graciously pleased to approve the award of the George Medal to the under mentioned:

23056357 Warrant Officer Class II Stephen David HAMBROOK, Corps of Royal Engineers.

Warrant Officer II Hambrook has been employed as Squadron Sergeant Major in Bomb Disposal since September 1968. During this time he has personally dealt with some 200 missiles and ten bombs. On three occasions he displayed outstanding courage.

In August 1969 he was in charge of a team excavating in search of a buried bomb near Petworth, Because of the particularly wet and marshy conditions specialised pumping equipment had to be in continuous use to prevent the excavation from flooding.

On 9th August a German 250 kilogram bomb was found and a No. 17 clockwork fuze identified in excellent condition. This type of fuze is particularly dangerous as the clock which had stopped can be re-started by any shock, and can then explode the bomb in a matter of seconds. The bomb could not be blown up where it lay because of the proximity of dwellings.

Sergeant Major Hambrook summoned the assistance of an officer and these two then arranged for the complete evacuation from the area of everyone but themselves.

Because of the noise made by the pumping sets (which could not be stopped without the risk of immediate flooding and collapse of the shaft), it was impossible to use the electronic stethoscope. Therefore there would have been no warning if the clock had re-started ticking at any time during the operation.

After the fuze was immunised the base plate of the bomb was removed. This revealed that the powder explosive filling had deteriorated to such an extent that some two gallons of nitro-glycerine (an exceedingly unstable explosive) had been formed and that the remaining 200lbs of powder was floating in it as lumps or sticking to the casing. This combination could only be removed by hand.

Apart from the extreme risk of explosion which could be caused by any small shock or friction, working conditions were made appalling by the fumes which cause constant retching and nausea. By the time the explosive had been removed Sergeant Major Hambrook had worked continuously for twenty-nine hours without rest or warm food, and had been exposed to extreme danger for eleven hours.

On 1st October 1969 Warrant Officer II Hambrook as second in command to his Squadron Commander was called to deal with a German Parachute Mine in London. This mine, which was found on a congested building site, contained over 1,500 lbs of Hexamite explosive and was of a type normally fitted with any combination of detonating devices sensitive to light, sound and metal tools as well as containing a clockwork delay mechanism.

It was decided that the devices could not be exposed and neutralised because of the prolonged risk to many people this procedure would cause. Therefore the explosive was removed by steam from the mine with the detonating systems still intact. This involved few people but greater risk due to the uncertain effects of steam and extreme changes of temperature on the devices, any of which could have caused an immediate explosion.

Warrant Office II Hambrook was required to assist in operating the steam generators and removing the explosive. He had to approach the mine at intervals never greater than half an hour throughout a period of some twelve hours.

On 11th December 1969 Warrant Officer II Hambrook was second in command of a team called to deal with a 500 kilogram German bomb at Fleet. This bomb was found to be fitted with a type 17 clockwork fuze and type 50 anti-disturbance fuze. This combination of fuzes was specifically designed to kill Bomb Disposal personnel.

Warrant Officer II Hambrook and the Troop Commander together fitted a magnetic clock stopper and immunised both fuzes. This task involved three hours of extremely dangerous work.

These are three examples of the skill, calmness and gallantry displayed by Warrant Officer II Hambrook.

His example has been an inspiration to other members of the Bomb Disposal Unit.

⊕ ⊕ ⊕

Later that month I was told that I had been selected as the Army's Man of the Year. There was another overwhelming press call and I was invited to dine at the Savoy Hotel where a presentation would take place, attended by previous Men of the Year and guests who paid £2,500 for the privilege, although I expect many of the tables were for corporate guests. It was a very pleasant evening during which my citation was read out and I was presented with a Man of the Year certificate and welcomed by the other Men of the Year into their exclusive club. I took a friend from the unit, another Sergeant Major, but I don't recall who else was on the table. The food was splendid.

Going to Buckingham Palace for the presentation of the George Medal was a tremendous experience and I was accompanied by my wife and mother. I was fortunate in that the presentation was made by Her Majesty Queen Elizabeth. She was shorter than I thought she would be, and petite. She was well informed and her composure and attitude was very relaxing for the recipients. I was in awe but very much enjoyed it, as did my wife and mother. Having changed from my uniform we then met up with work friends and spent the rest of that day enjoying ourselves at a club. I was embarrassed because one of my friends told the compere about my award and he announced it and everyone began to applaud. So I looked around pretending I didn't know they were applauding me. Some days later I learned that in the midst of the celebrating, my mother had experienced disappointment. Apparently she had told her friends that she would bring each of them a piece of royal toilet paper but when she went into the toilet she found that the paper was normal government issue, no royal crowns or ciphers.

The BBC were making a TV series of unusual happenings under the title of Those Who Dare and decided that one episode would be a re-enactment of the parachute mine incident at Chalk Farm. Filming was at a site in Kent and it was 10 days before the director was satisfied and our lives returned to normal. I was invited to the BBC TV studios to view the first screening. It was very good and I was given a copy on tape. When it was shown on television the episode caused much interest and I did several local press and radio interviews. One viewer wrote to the newspaper to say that it was obvious that it was a remake as Sergeant Major Hambrook did not have sweat on his brow.

Thirty Three

HAVING served over two years in the Bomb Disposal Squadron, I received a posting order as senior military instructor to the Royal Engineer Diving School at Marchwood in Hampshire. This was a promotion to Warrant Officer Class One. We were allocated a very comfortable house in a nice area about four miles from the school. Marchwood was also the home port for the Royal Engineer Maritime Fleet which, using their Fleet Auxiliary vessels, shipped stores for British bases in other countries.

The school was well equipped with static and mobile diving tanks, a compression chamber and diving equipment. This included standard equipment which would be used in fast flowing water where it would be dangerous to use scuba-style sets because the current could crush the breathing tubes.

It was a busy life with aptitude testing, continuation training and basic diving courses of four weeks running continuously. There was also frequent contact with the Royal Navy diving school at HMS *Vernon* in Portsmouth dockyard. Submarine escape was taught to submariners using a vertical tank that was 100 feet tall. Every month or so we were able to partake in this. It was quite an amazing experience. You went in at the base into a sealed unit, at normal atmospheric pressure. Once inside, the water is let in, gradually increasing the pressure. You are wearing a nose clip and when the pressure is equal the chamber is opened and you step into the tank and make your way towards the surface. At 20 feet intervals there are alcoves with instructors inside and they give you a quick punch to ensure you are breathing out and won't get an embolism. It was quite an experience.

One civilian employee was Sam Stanley, a former Royal Navy diving instructor, who supervised diving along with our team. Naval diving instructors are famed throughout the diving world for their hardness and apparent lack of concern for student diver's comfort. Sam, a particularly famed kind heart, had some army diving officers on a continuation course. One came to the surface without signalling or warning and was obviously in a panic. He pulled his face mask off shouting, "Help, I'm drowning."

"And a very good job you are making of it, Sir," replied our Sam.

During the summer of 1972, the Junior Leaders Regiment's sub-aqua club were going to the south of France for three weeks of diving and I was invited. I took my wife, who was pregnant at the time, and the diving promised to be good. Unfortunately, the water was grossly contaminated and many of us suffered upset stomachs that lasted for days and made us feel exhausted. Despite this, a daily routine of a morning and afternoon dive followed by the recharging of the air cylinders and a relaxed evening was established. During one dive, close to an onshore wartime fort, we found an incomplete gun barrel about nine feet in length, possibly 88 millimetres calibre. We decided to recover it as a trophy for the Junior Leaders. The easiest way to get it ashore was to use diving nylon safety lines hooked onto a Land Rover to pull it ashore in stages. This worked very well and we got quite a surprise when, in less than a foot of water, a large conger eel emerged and swam off. The barrel was taken back to England and mounted outside of the Junior Leaders diving club. I assume that when the area was overrun by the Allies they had blown up this gun.

During our time in France, an Englishman and his teenage son attempted to climb down a 60 foot high cliff to a small sandy cove. The father fell and the distressed son clambered down to him, where he waited, shouting for help. He was heard by other residents of the camp who came to us. The quickest way of reaching them was by water, so we rapidly carried the inflatable and out board motor to a nearby beach and motored through the rough sea to the cove. The man was dead and the boy very distressed. We took him back to the beach we'd come from and the ladies from among the campers looked after him whilst the local emergency services recovered his father's body. Later that evening the campsite residents raised £7,000 to help the distressed family.

During diver training we practised rolling over the side of an inflatable dinghy at speed, following each other into the water in rapid sequence. One day our non-diving Quarter Master Sergeant, Andy, asked if he could join in. Several days later he joined us. He was put into a dry diving suit and had the procedure explained to him. In addition, he would be the last to roll over the side giving him the opportunity to watch everyone else.

Following each other on the supervisor's orders, the sequence was simple. You step from the boat into an inflatable dinghy lashed alongside, then lay along its gunwale and roll over the side – all in a matter of seconds. The drop off progressed until it was Andy's turn at which point he somehow, while rolling off, got his legs tangled in the cordage lashing the dinghy to the boat. He was dragged along at a fast rate of knots, head and shoulders under the water, his legs kicking wildly in the air to the sound of belly laughs all round. Andy was rescued but not before his diving suit and stomach was full of water. Andy's cryptic comments on divers and their training were a revelation and never again did we manage to get him into a diving suit and the water!

Thirty Four

IN 1972, our twins – Samantha and Daniell were born. My wife's three were now at boarding schools because they were at the age where my postings and our frequent house moves were disrupting their education. That same year the British diving officer with the Gurkha Squadron in Hong Kong died in a diving accident and together with four other instructors I flew to Hong Kong to retrain the diving team. Our accommodation was a rundown barracks next to a vast slaughter house which was continually butchering pigs imported from China. The very loud and unending squealing of the pigs was more than intrusive.

It was hot and muggy and throughout the six weeks we were there, the underwater visibility was nil. It was unnerving when unidentifiable creatures swam past, brushing our bodies. The Gurkha Sappers were hard working and friendly and readily accepted our instruction. We were invited to a party during which a pig was slaughtered and used in a curry. There was music and dancing but only the men danced, with the wives watching. It was an unusual evening but a pleasant one.

There was a British yacht club in the garrison and we were asked to provide safety cover for a regatta. A standard army assault boat fitted with a powerful outboard motor was loaned to us for the day. During the racing a very strong wind blew up. Those that could get to shore did so. Others we towed into sheltered waters but one that was far out was swept from sight towards the border with China. We set out along the coast to search, hoping to find it before we reached the estuary that divided Hong Kong from China. Eventually, we spotted it, beached on the Chinese coast.

Ensuring that the two sailors in it were all right, apart from being cold, and having secured a tow rope to the dinghy, we freed it from the sand, took the sailors into our boat and set off, towing it back to the club. The wind was still strong, the sea was choppy and torrential rain fell for the two hours it took us to get back to the club where the sun was shining and a barbecue was taking place. It was not an experience that I would wish to repeat.

We were taken to the colony's Chinatown for a very interesting sightseeing visit and then to the seaside esplanade about 25 feet above the rocky shore. Directly beneath on the rocks lay the bodies of several elderly Chinese. They had committed suicide by throwing themselves onto the rocks because they were expected to contribute to the family but could no longer do so.

Near the end of our stay the Gurkhas put on a special meal and drinks for us. It had been six weeks of hard work but very enjoyable.

Back at the school life went on as before except that we were now taking students to Wyke Regis near Weymouth to practise fast water searching and night attack techniques. About this time I was awarded the Army's Long Service and Good Conduct Medal for 18 years exemplary service.

An interesting diving task that came up was when a team of scientists from a military establishment needed us to retrieve pieces of, and sometimes whole, Rapier surface to air missiles which had been launched from a firing range out over the sea. They were aimed at towed targets, similar to the banners you see being pulled behind planes. It's a very effective missile but contained in capsules attached to their noses was a radioactive substance that reacted with a receiver in the target to signify a hit. There were concerns that this substance might be damaging marine life, especially since buildings on the range had been contaminated by capsules on mounted missiles dissolving when it rained and being carried into the buildings on staff footwear. Because of this, the building had been demolished with the debris sealed in drums and taken for deep sea dumping – a huge operation.

The range was situated on a small chain of connected islands off the port of Oban and we arrived by ferry to be briefed. The recovery area was three miles offshore. Our accommodation was in the former Sergeants' mess which was sparsely furnished. It was agreed that our fully charged diving sets would be taken aboard and when all had been used we would return them to the former range harbour for recharging for the following day. There was no land between America and these islands and the Atlantic Ocean was a fretful beast. The rollers hit our narrow beamed launch making it difficult to dive from, so our inflatable, where the diving attendants sat, was lashed alongside with divers going in and out of the water from there.

The visibility was excellent but the water depth was at the limit since the divers were limited to 10 metres. Others with different qualifications could go almost twice as deep and myself and one other could go even deeper. The surface swell was moving at the same depth as the water, 100 feet, and with seaweed swaying with the swell it was possible to feel seasickness at depth. I have never felt so sick in all my life.

The dry suits we were using had a small capacity auxiliary air cylinder fitted at waist level. This was turned on and off by the user to combat the pressure creasing of the suit. It was not possible to lay a search pattern as the location of fallen missiles and their fragments was only known to be within a mile of the shore. The diver was guided by rope signals from his surface attendant who often felt quite unwell. The scientists on board had tablets fastened behind their ears. These seemed to allay sickness. On the second day fragments were being recovered and ideally these would have been placed in a net and hauled to the surface by those on the launch. As it turned out there was none available and this would have been too dangerous in any case due to the swell. The items were light so when a diver had collected all he could manage, he would return to the surface with them. This meant that the individual's air supply did not last as long because the rise from the deepest depth meant a three minute decompression stop 30 feet below the surface, before completing the ascent. The deeper you go, the air you're breathing is of a higher pressure, the pressure of the surrounding water, and if you dive beyond the depth at which decompression on resurfacing is necessary, the high pressure in your blood and lungs will rupture your lungs. This is known as an air embolism. You have to stop at various pre-planned stages to allow your blood to stabilise. We didn't have depth gauges and indicating ropes weren't possible, so it was a case of the attendant pulling in the line and when he estimated the right depths, he gave a tug on the rope. There is a system of communication – four pulls means come up now, four pulls and two bells or quick tugs from the diver means I need to come up, help me up. Those three minutes when you're waiting underwater going through decompression is a very long time but you get used to it.

On returning to the shore the rolling sensation continued and made you sway all night. In the evening our sets were recharged with air using portable compressors. From my bomb disposal experience, I was concerned that handling the missile fragments, some of which were radioactive, might contaminate the divers so I made them keep their diving suits on until we were back in the accommodation and could be showered off, still in their suits.

I was diving and searching close to my depth limit when I saw an intact missile lying in a fairly deep depression in the sea bed. I resolved to recover it, did so, and signalled that I wanted to ascend to the surface with assistance. For some reason the signal was not acknowledged so I attempted to start my return to the surface only to find that I had no buoyancy. I was in danger of sinking so I opened my auxiliary air cylinder to find that it didn't contain enough air to overcome the depth pressure. I was close to running out of breathable air and the only thing I could do was to discard my weight belt and fin towards the surface. Slowly, I rose until the pressure lessened and the air in my suit expanded. This took me more quickly to the surface and I had to breathe out constantly to avoid an embolism. I vented my suit by putting my fingers inside the neck seal. In the other hand I carried the missile. I broke surface with a flurry of spray, handed the missile over then swam round the launch to the inflatable to find my attendant prostrate with seasickness. The task lasted eight working days before sufficient fragments and several intact missiles were recovered, enabling the scientists to complete their investigation.

When we deployed to Oban I mentioned to the naval divers the tablets that the scientists had taped behind their ears and the following morning when they paraded for the morning muster each had an aspirin taped to their forehead!

Another diving job was in Scotland where we were needed to establish a line for a water pipeline from Bo'ness near Falkirk to the opposite mainland 800 yards from Bo'ness across the Firth of Forth. We were staying in a territorial unit in Falkirk, cooking for ourselves and sleeping in the drill hall. When I observed the strip of water, or sound, between the two coasts, I saw that the rising and falling tides flowed at an average exceeding six knots. This would restrict our diving time to when there was slack water. We also saw an abundance of marine life, including whales, seals and dolphins – all of which broke the surface frequently. An initial test dive showed that there were massive kelp beds under which a diver would have to swim. To mark the line we made up heavy weights connected to empty but sealed 45 gallon oil drums. These acted as floats. During the first dive, 100 yards was checked and marked but the incoming tide made it dangerous to continue. At high tide I went to check on the markers and couldn't see them. At low water they came to the surface – they'd been swept to a depth where the water pressure had crushed them almost flat but fortunately they still marked the line. Diving went on from an inflatable Gemini dinghy. It became more difficult as we moved into thicker kelp which interfered with the diver's safety line and progress along the seabed to the point where the safety lines themselves were a danger. I decided we would dive without them but in pairs so that no one would be underwater alone. This worked well and with the underwater reconnaissance complete, we enjoyed several days relaxing before loading our equipment and making the long and boring drive back to the unit.

Thirty Five

A S MY time at the school came to an end, I was informed that I had been selected to be commissioned. I was very pleased and went to Headquarters Royal Engineers at Chatham to be measured by a Moss Bros representative for mess dress. I would wear this for the ceremony and then parade and special events. Mess dress consisted of a scarlet jacket, waistcoat and cummerbund and tight, black trousers with a red stripe. On September 25, 1973, I became Lieutenant Hambrook RE GM.

After a short commissioning course I was told that my posting, which was accompanied, would be to 29 Field Squadron Royal Engineers in Hamelin. My wife, the twins and I flew to RAF Gutersloh and onto what would be our home for the next three years – a large and very comfortable house in a leafy suburb of Hamelin. All the houses in the street were occupied by British officers. The boys would come out during their school holidays.

Two weeks after I arrived in Germany, I was flown back to England and to the Royal Armoured Corps station at Bovington near Basingstoke. I was to spend three weeks learning about the armoured personnel carrier that would be the standard means of transportation in my new unit. I also had to learn to drive the 17-tonne beast over undulating ground, although I took my test through a Weymouth packed with holiday makers. Very exhilarating! Back in Bovington, I was told that I had passed and was the holder of a tracked vehicle license. I took the opportunity to visit my mother in Brighton then flew back to Germany. Some years before I was sent to a suspected bomb in Hartington Cemetery, behind my mother's house. It wasn't a bomb fortunately. I called in to see her then too.

The Officers' mess had a vibrant social life which we enjoyed to the full. At regimental dinners it was customary for men to escort the lady who would be sat at their left to the dining table. This ensured that one ended up on the opposite side to one's wife or partner. During one dinner my wife was seated next to a senior officer who had a diver qualification badge on his uniform sleeve. On seeing this she asked him to tell her about his diving experiences. He did, then went on, sufficiently loudly for me to hear, about a training exercise which involved diving to recover inert demolition charges strapped underwater to a jetty. He had run short of air and surfaced without giving the correct signals. Clinging to the jetty edge, his instructor told him to go back down and follow the correct surfacing procedure. To emphasise the point, the instructor trod on his fingers to make him let go of the jetty.

"How terrible. Who would do such a thing?" asked my wife.

The officer pointed across the table at me. "Him."

The field exercises we undertook in Germany included watermanship, bridging and mine clearance among other things and although they were fairly frequent they were not overlong and I was able to keep my diving qualifications in date.

After six months in Germany the unit flew to Ballykelly, a former RAF airfield near Londonderry in Northern Ireland, for four months. We were needed as the backup engineer unit to supply resources. It was a strange experience especially because the Republican movement was very active. To avoid becoming a target whenever our Land Rover stopped at traffic lights, we had to get out, weapons in hand, and scan passing civilians, in case they were the enemy. It was daunting but part of the job.

I became a civilian liaison officer, essentially the friendly face of the British Army, and did not wear a uniform for much of the time. I was given a Mini to drive. It was supposed to be incognito but there was an army fire extinguisher inside so I chucked that in the boot. Sometime later, when I was driving into the diving club, I showed the guard my ID and he jumped back and saluted me. Cover blown, just like that. I had a not so quiet word with the guy and tried to change my car but I had to go back to being an officer in charge of the support troop. I continued with one of my duties, which was to engage with the Port Rush diving club that met in the Harbour Inn. There was great deep diving in the area, especially around Rathlin Island. I made lots of friends and it was good for us engineer divers to widen our experience and continue our process of registering dives in our log books.

One evening in the inn, a man came towards me and said, "What the hell are you doing here?"

He continued to be aggressive and threatening. I told him to go away but he didn't and the landlady stepped in and told him to back off, that I was her kissing cousin and that he and his mates should remember that. So I came under her protection.

I also commanded the Support Troop which was kept busy supplying the Field Troop sections with their various needs. A corporal plant operator was crushed to death when the forklift truck he was driving overturned pinning him beneath but this was our only casualty of the tour.

The police requested that our diving team search a river bed into which a suspect, on being challenged, had thrown a shotgun. This was a combined police and army operation with the police providing our security. The river was about 40 yards wide and slow moving but with no visibility and a very muddy bottom. A search scheme was laid out and diving began. We had to grope along the bottom from bank to bank. It was difficult as there were large lumps of slimy material in the water but on the third search lane I touched metal, felt around it, and realised that it was the dumped shotgun. Carefully lifting it, I returned to the bank and gave the gun to the police. I then asked about the slimy material and was told it was probably waste from a small slaughter house upstream. My find meant that I was a witness for the police. I returned to Germany for a fortnight's leave, which I enjoyed with Angela and the children, then it was back to routine exercises and duties on camp for a few weeks before I returned to Northern Ireland. After landing in Belfast I stayed on HMS *Belfast*, which was being used as transit accommodation. On the day of the trial at Belfast Crown Court I was taken to the witness waiting room which I quickly realised I was sharing with supporters of the charged man. It was a very uncomfortable situation and in the end the accused pleaded guilty and I wasn't needed. I went back to HMS *Belfast* and several days later returned to Hamelin. In 1974 I was awarded the General Service Medal (Northern Ireland clasp) for my tour of duty there.

Thirty Six

MY FAMILY and I spent three years in Germany before I was posted back to the Royal Engineer Combat Diving School in Kiel which as a Quarter Master Sergeant Instructor I had formed 10 years previously. I was returning as the Officer Commanding in the rank of Captain. Once again, it was an accompanied posting and we were allocated a nice house in a quiet cul-de-sac where the other houses were occupied by officers from various services and nations. The twins were enrolled into a local German kindergarten where, despite being the only English children, they were happy and quickly picked up the language.

Once again I formed an alliance with the German engineers at Rendsburg and soon we were having joint diving exercises and sharing social activities whilst having a steady stream of divers coming through the school on courses, some of whom were Canadian. The exercises were made as realistic as possible with tough physical training and night diving to clear purpose-laid inert mines and inert demolition charges. Winter lasts up to six months in the Baltic area with the sea being frozen for at least half of that but this made no difference to the training apart from us being unable to leave the harbour. The term harbour usually means a man-made structure but only the German fleet had use of them. The yacht club was an inlet which had a permanently open end giving access to the Baltic. Sometimes I stayed overnight in their Officers' mess and was amused by the breakfast arrangements as at 6am a single boiled egg was placed at each laid place together with two slices of buttered bread and a small carton of jam. I was used to being served my meal and therefore eating it piping hot but it was explained to me that the German services had a rule that said the same rations were to be served to all ranks at every meal. They all wore the same uniforms too. I think it was something that had been enforced at the end of the Second World War.

On a shared training exercise with the German engineer divers we were aboard a landing craft which took us to an area where munitions of all kinds were dumped at the end of the war. This made for interesting diving and our host divers were intent on recovering the largest shells in order to disconnect the shell from its case, throw the shell and propellant from the case back into the sea, and sell the recovered brass casings for scrap – hence the need for the largest ones. We participated fully in the recovery of the munitions but I was somewhat surprised to see the shells being detached from their casing with hacksaws. My bomb disposal experience made me cautious of this and just as I was expressing my concern to the senior diver there was a sudden hissing, loud and growing louder, coming from a shell that had just been cut into. The engineer doing the cutting moved pretty quickly at which point, I ran across to the shell, picked it up and threw it overboard. Almost immediately its propellant exploded. My concerns had been dramatically proven correct and my fingers scorched from the hot shell casing. The diving continued but no more dumped munitions were recovered.

On Remembrance Day we paraded at the Allied War Memorial on the outskirts of Kiel. We also laid the traditional poppy wreaths.

Kiel University had a sub-aqua (diving) club which used the university swimming pool and I was asked if our instructors would help to train the members. This was agreed and twice a week we met at the pool for training and went afterwards for drinks. This led to some interesting friendships. The divers had their own club but often attended functions at the yacht club and there were formal events at the British Officers' mess in Kiel. It was a busy life both on and off duty. The social life was very vibrant and, being a small close knit unit, unfortunately some relationships were formed which caused stress to those who cared, and were accepted by those who did not.

After two years at Kiel, I received a posting as the Quartermaster of 24 Field Squadron based in Kitchener Barracks in Gillingham, Kent. It was at this time that Angela told me she was leaving me for my Commanding Officer. He lived three doors away from us. I was upset, particularly as she planned to take the girls, then aged four, with her. But these things happen and there was no chance of reconciliation. Some months later she returned to England to take her other children out of boarding school and settled with her partner in Sussex.

My role in my new post was to keep the unit supplied so that it could function as an operational Field Squadron in the UK and abroad. This could be tedious and fairly routine but my accommodation in the Brompton Barracks Officers' mess was good. I had a large semi-basement room comfortably furnished, which opened out onto a paved area. I soon gained access to the twins who I picked up every other Saturday morning and returned to Goring on Sunday evenings. There were no motorways then so the journey took about three hours but we enjoyed ourselves playing I-Spy and singing songs. Lord Of The Dance is one I recall. I have never spoken badly of my former wives to my children as they would only despise me for it. They can make up their mind on matters later.

At first when I had the girls, we stayed at my mother's home in Brighton. But some months later I got permission for them to stay in my accommodation in Brompton. My bat-woman – an army term for paid help – was a genial elderly lady who made the girls feel welcome, which was pleasing for all of us.

During this time the Americans planned to visit Brompton Barracks and on the day of their arrival three Chinook helicopters swung into the skies and banked over the nearby married quarters. There followed a tremendous down draft that blew all the washing off the lines, distributed it across the gardens and stripped every young tree of its branches. The Chinooks then landed on our parade ground and the troops and vehicles streamed out, driving off the square and out of the barrack gates, presumably to report their arrival. But that was where they stopped, spluttering to a halt having forgotten that they had drained their fuel tanks as a pre-flight safety precaution.

The Americans were our guests for two weeks, living with us but eating their own rations cooked in our kitchen by their chef. At the end of the fortnight there was to be a formal parade of both units. When that day came our unit, dressed in parade uniform – officers complete with swords – formed up on the drill square while the Americans formed up on the road in front of the accommodation block. They were going to march on and halt facing us. When the time came for the American unit to march we heard the command to march immediately followed by a single voice chanting, "We are off to war" followed by all repeating this and also the next line, "With a dirty whore." I had to quickly turn to tell the men that, difficult as it was, they must stop laughing. When formed up facing each other, we in parade uniform and the Americans in working dress, the formalities of parting were quickly conducted and later that day the Chinook helicopters returned. This time the occupants of the married quarters had been warned and there was no washing to be seen.

Thirty Seven

DURING this time we deployed as a unit to participate in a NATO engineering exercise in Germany. We were to cross the channel on the normal cross channel ferries and, as no weapons were allowed to be carried, all weapons were placed in the back of a standard 4-tonne truck and the canopy opening firmly lashed closed. Myself and a Staff Sergeant were to drive and safeguard its load which made me uneasy as on the ferry the vehicles are left unattended. Our vehicle would be a prime target for criminals wanting to steal arms. Determined that this would not happen I armed us both with a pistol and ammunition and we slept, or tried to sleep, in the vehicle cab. The ferry docked early the next morning with our load safe and intact and our vehicles and men disembarked and started the long drive to the exercise area. The exercise was three weeks long, after which we returned to the UK.

Living in the Officers' mess was comfortable but after the day's work one would change into a suit, meet at the mess bar, have a drink or two then go into dine, perhaps having wine with the meal. Some men were happy with this but I could see evidence that some of them were becoming quite institutionalised. I realised that this could easily happen to me and that I'd end up spending my salary and have nothing to show for it. Having made up my mind what to do, I looked for, and bought, a semi-detached four bedroom house with a garage, and a small front and large back garden in Sittingbourne. The house was fairly cheap because a divorcing couple had trashed the interior – presumably to deny each other money – and left it in a filthy condition. Even the carpet tiles in the lounge seemed to wriggle and I sprayed them with a strong disinfectant a couple of days before I moved in. I can't understand people like that.

I cleaned the main bedroom, put in a sleeping bag and air mattress and made it my base. I wasn't bothered where I was sleeping as I was pleased to be on the property ladder. Then, starting in the lounge, I ripped up the carpet tiles and took them to the tip. I cleaned where they had laid and moved on to the kitchen which needed the units replacing and all appliances. Fortunately, I have very good DIY skills and after several weeks of me spending all of my spare hours working on the house, during which time the girls and I stayed at my mother's on their weekends, I was able to cook a meal. Now it was time to redecorate. A local carpet layer helped me to choose carpets and a fellow officer's wife offered to buy the furniture, curtains and bedding. This was a great help to me as the unit was to deploy on a BAOR exercise for three weeks. I drew cash out of the bank and gave it to her and left all choices to her discretion. When I got back, the house finally looked like a home and that weekend having picked up the twins, I was able to introduce them to the house and their twin bedroom. The girls were as pleased and excited as I was, especially as the house backed onto farm fields and had plenty of local play areas. They made friends with a young girl living next door and together they played outdoors, or inside if the weather was bad. I bought a Yamaha 250cc motor cycle to make my journey to and from the unit, especially during the rush hour, much quicker.

Once again my current tour was coming to an end and I received a posting to the Defence Explosive Ordnance (bomb disposal) School where I had previously served as an instructor. I was returning as the Senior Army Instructor and second in command and with the school being about 27 miles from my home I had no problem with daily commuting. It was a post that I enjoyed, being involved more in technical matters and occasionally instructing in subjects of which I have specialist knowledge. In August 1980, during my first year in the post I flew to America and, having evaded the begging Moonies at the airport, stayed in a hotel in Washington as a guest of the FBI. I was allocated an agent as a guide and taken on a VIP tour of the FBI headquarters, the Senate, House of Representatives and the White House. I was intrigued to discover that they were all connected by an underground tracked rail system so that authorised personnel didn't need to go outside. I was somewhat amused to note that all of the agents were dressed in remarkably similar clothing and wore a lapel badge stating Secret Service. I was warned not to go to certain downtown areas alone or after dark.

After a week I was flown down to Redstone Arsenal in Tennessee to the United States Missile and Munitions School. On arrival I was taken to a car hire depot and loaned an air conditioned car for the duration of my stay. I was also given a fully equipped, self catering, bachelor officer flat within the Arsenal perimeter. I did any shopping needed at the PX store, which is the American equivalent of the British Navy Army Air Force Institute, or NAAFI. The choice was wide and bewildering, even the milk came in many flavours other than plain. I was issued with an American working uniform which I packed to pass on to my sons and carried on wearing my British uniform.

It was extremely hot and the working day was from 5am, with a breakfast of creamed mincemeat just after 6am. We went on until noon when all were stood down and then worked again from 3pm to around 6pm. Most lunch times I stayed in the school building and changed into running kit before jogging along the range roads for about an hour then back to the school to strip off and squat in a cleaner's sink to wash in cold water before changing back into my uniform. To dry any washing I had hung a string between the two rear windows of my car. It dried by the time I finished work each day. The flat was well laid out and the kitchen nicely equipped. Some of it wasn't familiar to me. I was happy with a diet of eggs and salad on most days but one day, when having hard boiled eggs, I put them into the kitchen sink to cool down and having wondered what a black button on the side was for, pressed it to find out. There was an immediate grinding noise and my eggs disappeared through the sink waste grinder. My curiosity was satisfied but my hunger was not.

My role while in America was to teach the disposal of chemical weapons on live drums. There were many on the base and some of them were leaking. The American protective clothing consisted of thick heavy rubber all-in-one suits with cheek pad respirator filters. These were many years behind the lightweight disposable suits and respirators developed by the Research Establishment at Porton Down and in use throughout the British Army.

On site it was necessary to be constantly hosed down in an effort to cool down. It was difficult to work and on starting we were told that someone would always pass out causing the instructor to give injections of nerve gas antidote in case this was due to breathing in deadly fumes. I was given a weapon to work on and with time found that I felt nauseous. I also noticed that the instructor seemed to be hovering close to me and asking repeatedly if I was all right. My diving experience helped me to overcome the feeling of sickness and to regain control of my breathing. When my task was complete I went to the decontamination point and was hosed down, stripped of the suit and directed to the shower to complete the process. I later examined some of the cheek pad filters, including the ones I wore, and found that mine had a distinctly different odour to the others. I realised that this was a deliberate act to cause a student to be sick or to panic, and to show the students what the outcome of the nerve agent could be. This made me very angry because if I hadn't been used to overcoming sickness at depth as a diver, I would have pulled the helmet off and been exposed to the chemicals. I had been invited there as an expert, so this was hugely disrespectful. Maybe they resented my going there.

I spoke to the supervising Warrant Officer about this and he said "Yes, and we thought you did very well not to go under." I did not reply but contrary to the Military Code I punched him hard in the face. He wouldn't report me because the reason for my punch would have been revealed and he would have been in trouble.

Some of the disposal techniques would not have been used by the UK teams and the use of explosives was veering on the dangerous; an example of this was when I saw a detonator being placed into the bulk charge. This should be the last thing done but having prepared a drum of chemical agent and put that into a hole that had been dug on top of fuel soaked kindling and logs of wood for destruction by burning, the instructor, having gathered the students around the hole then placed the detonator into the plastic explosive charge. He then invited one to take it from him and place it on the drum. At this point, together with two Australian engineers who had received the same UK training as me, I moved backwards. Later we were asked why and explained what we considered to be the only safe way to use explosives.

On completion of my time at Redstone Arsenal I had a few days local leave and visited American service friends in Tennessee. I returned to the UK via Washington to resume my duties at the school and soon afterwards I was promoted to Major. I was very pleased.

Thirty Eight

ABOUT this time my former wife decided that she did not want the responsibility for the twins and I applied to the court for full custody. They came home with me from the hearing. There was a very good school, the Convent of St Mary, about a mile from our home, and the twins became paying pupils there. I looked for and found a live-in nanny who was young and got on well with my daughters.

This worked and we were happy.

After buying and renovating my house I met a local divorcee, Gill, who had a five-year-old son called Morris. He often stayed at my home and the children became firm friends. Gill and I enjoyed long cross country walks especially along the North Downs Way, the Pilgrims Way and along the banks of the River Medway to Maidstone. We would walk up to 20 miles a day and because the lower countryside was interlaced by fresh water streams, we often took buttered bread and salt and cut the growing watercress to make sandwiches for lunch.

In 1982 I returned to America to attend the Naval Explosive Ordnance Disposal Unit at Indian Head, Maryland. This was a fascinating experience. I took samples of the British chemical and biological protection suit and of the then current S6 Respirator with me and demonstrated these to a gathering of service and civilian scientists and left the samples with them. I also met up with a friend I had made during my previous visit who owned a restored motor launch. He took me out on the Mississippi River cruising from one riverside attraction to another, a great way to see the riverside townships.

At the school, life was as busy as before with students of varying nationalities on various levels of training. Then, in 1982, the British Falkland Islands were invaded and occupied by Argentina. This provoked an immediate response from Britain and a force was sent to retake them, which they did after 10 weeks of intense fighting on land, sea and in the air. There was much clearance work to be done afterwards and this required experienced personnel who would serve for six months.

Gill and I found our relationship deepening and we became a close couple, which was extremely pleasing for us all. She had her own home not too far from mine so meeting and sharing was relatively easy. When I was warned that I might be deployed to the Falklands, she proposed to me. I accepted and, a few days later, she produced a special licence including a date for the wedding. It took me totally by surprise but I was pleased because it meant the children would have a mother to look after them. We married in the local registry office with witnesses only and didn't go on honeymoon as my deployment date was getting close. Gill and the children would live in my house as a family while I was away so the nanny was thanked for her services and left the home for another appointment.

Thirty Nine

I DO consider myself a sentimental person but I didn't take any photographs of my children with me when I was deployed. I always carried a rosary with me in my pocket though. As a child I attended Sunday School in Shoreham, at the Baptist church although we were a Church of England family. When I was in my early 20s I found that I wasn't getting what I needed in terms of mental support from the Baptists so I underwent the training and converted to Roman Catholicism, which I found very rewarding. The rosary I was given then was in my trouser pocket always.

This was the case when in October 1982 I went to the Falkland Islands to command the clearance operations. It was a daunting task with much explosive ordnance and many mines scattered across the islands. The defeated troops had booby trapped various discarded items and there were fatal casualties arising from these. I had a feeling that something might happen to me and that it might be my left leg, but I had had those feelings before.

Having taken over the detachment, in my office among the other documents and records I examined, were the RAF photographs of bombs that had been dropped by the RAF on and around Stanley airfield. I concluded that at least nine had not exploded. Later that week I took a section and worked along the line shown in the plates. I uncovered and collected the shattered remains of seven in one day. These had broken up on impact but they hadn't been armed when they were dropped so we didn't need to detonate them. We unscrewed the fuzes and set fire to the explosive. Two deeply buried bombs were located and logged for later recovery. It was a good day's work. The section was accommodated in two empty bungalows and I was a lodger in a third. Christmas came and went. It was low key but we celebrated as best we could and I presented a framed picture to the local couple, Chick and Walter, who were our landlords. I'd brought it with me from the UK. In early January the BBC broadcast Songs of Praise programme from Stanley Cathedral.

The following was written by the author Ralph Barker for inclusion in my resume of service. I'm not sure why he wrote it, I received it in the post one day. This was an incident that occurred three months into my deployment in the Falklands.

◈ ◈ ◈

"One 1,000 pound bomb, colour green, no tail unit, no apparent impact damage, lying three degrees from the horizontal. The nose is pointed towards the control tower of Stanley airfield. It's approximately one thousand two hundred yards south of the control tower. It's fitted with a tail pistol, and I can just see the kidney plate."

Confronting Steve Hambrook, the Royal Engineer's Major directing bomb disposal operations in the Falklands, was a live weapon similar to the one that had already obliterated a colleague. His task, as his colleague's had been, was to make it safe.

Cold-blooded, they called it. And it was true, you had to be a bit more than deadpan. But Hambrook was no iceberg. His blood was as warm as the next man's.

Digging gingerly around the exposed tail of the unexploded bomb, every nerve end alerted, 48 year old Steve Hambrook was intent on recording every detail of the weapon beside which he was kneeling, and of the step-by-step measures he proposed to take to defuse it. Then, if anything went wrong, his successors would have something to work on.

Eight months earlier, in May of that same year, 1982, at the height of the Falklands campaign, a similar general purpose bomb had hit the frigate HMS *Antelope* and lodged in her engine room without exploding. For many hours two Royal Engineer NCOs, Staff Sergeant Jim Prescott and Sergeant Major John Phillips had worked in the engine room under battle conditions in an effort to save the ship. But during the night, for some unexplained reason, the bomb had exploded, killing Prescott and maiming Phillips, and precipitating the loss of the Antelope.

Inevitably, Steve Hambrook had that incident very much in mind as he parted the sandy soil of Stanley airfield, eroded by recent high winds, and uncovered the rear end of the bomb.

Judging from the apparent angle of the impact, the bomb had been dropped from low level. But not so low there had not been time for the tiny propeller to spin sufficiently in flight to eject the arming forks, as it was designed to do, making the bomb live.

Why it hadn't gone off in the first place no one could tell. That was his problem. The precise state of its internal mechanism now was similarly uncertain.

An additional hazard facing the wiry, resilient Hambrook was the likely deterioration of the bomb's detonator after a lapse of eight months. The bomb must have been dropped in April or May, and it was now 29th December. Interaction with the explosive filling would meanwhile have formed a compound of crystals highly sensitive to friction.

In 28 years' experience of bomb disposal, much of it as a non-commissioned officer, Hambrook had dealt with more than 2,000 incidents proving his courage many times over, and he had a George Medal to show for it. Following work on an unexploded wartime German landmine in 1969, revealed during building excavations, he had had a block of flats in Kentish Town named after him, and in 1971 he had been voted the Army's Man of the Year. But as befitted a married man with four children, he was proud of his reputation for caution. Under normal conditions he would scarcely have contemplated the task he was about to attempt.

The safe method would be to pack fresh explosive on to the weapon and blow it up by remote control where it was. But such action, adjacent to the runway of Stanley airfield, and within fragmentation distance of parked aircraft, was not operationally acceptable.

Nor was it operationally acceptable to compromise the RAF's ability to react to an emergency – and hostilities had not been ended – by flying all the aircraft off while the bomb was exploded. Argentinean radar would have picked any such movement up and given them the chance to react aggressively.

One of Hambrook's sections, in the course of a clearance operation across the Stanley peninsula, had discovered the bomb that afternoon. Hambrook had been called from his office in Port Stanley, and after confirming the opinion of his NCO that they were dealing with a British general purpose thousand pounder, he suspended all other clearance work and directed the section to establish a cordon round the bomb at 300 metres to ensure that no one went near it.

By four o'clock Hambrook was conferring with Headquarters British Forces Falkland Islands and the RAF to arrange the least inconvenient time for clearing the area and closing the airfield. "How long will the job take you?" he was asked.

"For the actual defusing, better give me half an hour".

A span of 20:00 to 20:30 hours was chosen, giving Hambrook time to call in his standby sections to replace the men who had worked through the day, and to make his own preparations for tackling the bomb. By 19:00 hours he had returned to the site with his equipment – tool kit, two-way radio, tape recorder and so on. He had also studied the manual on this type of bomb. The instructions were as he remembered them, and they were unequivocal. No attempt to remove an armed pistol from this type of bomb should normally be made after it had been dropped. The bomb should be detonated in situ. As for the detonator, it should not be removed if it had been fitted for more than six days.

This spelt it out starkly enough. But this was not a normal situation. Full operational capacity had to be retained if at all possible.

The treeless sterility of the Stanley peninsula had rarely seemed so desolate to Hambrook as on this late December evening, with the strident activity of the airfield unnaturally silenced and stilled. The only movement to disturb him was the robot rotation of the radar dome straight ahead. The light, however, was good, and would remain so for at least two hours.

After a few minutes cautious, exploratory digging, Hambrook took a piece of cotton waste from his kit and began wiping the kidney-shaped plate fitted at the tail end of the bomb – the identification place on which were stamped the bomb's characteristics. Encrusted with sand and grime though it was, he could make out most of the hieroglyphics. He switched on the microphone he had plugged in to his mini recorder. "Start. Kidney-plate details." Now and again, even with the aid of a magnifying glass, he hesitated, and sometimes misread a figure before tracing the indentation with a pencil and correcting himself. "P.A.T. sixty...nine. Wrong – sixty-eight." Serial numbers, bomb weight, type, date and time of filling – all these and other details were laboriously spelt out, with occasional corrections. None of these details would be of much use to him personally, but an accurate record of them might be crucial to those who came after, if that was the way of it.

Finally, he turned to the tail pistol. This was the mechanical section that fired the detonator, which in turn fired the bomb. A circular chunk of metal, like a rather stubby piston, it protruded slightly from the rear end of the bomb case. (The tail unit itself had become detached from the bomb on impact).

In assembling this type of bomb, detonator and pistol were loaded separately, detonator first, then pistol. It was not like a fuzed bomb, where to take the fuze out was to remove the first part of the explosive train and render the bomb safe. With the pistol type, even after he had removed the pistol he would still have the detonator to contend with. He selected a pair of dividers and a ruler from his toolkit and measured the pistol across. "Tail pistol is of brass, and the diameter is 2.25 inches." This agreed with the manual. "The outside identification of the pistol is a British No. 78 tail pistol, and multi-way."

Whereas the bomb that penetrated to the engine room of the Antelope had been dropped by the Argentine Air Force, this one, he guessed, had probably been dropped at speed by a low flying Harrier, judging from its angle of entry. Even that, though, was speculation. In the past, British made armaments had been sold to Argentina, and it was one of the ironies of the campaign that in several instances the same weapons were used by both sides.

The bomb he was crouched over could well have been dropped by the Argies. Some devilish anti-handling device could have been fitted. All he could do was get on with the job.

"It is now 19:30 hours. The following have occurred." Just as well to confirm that it is all on tape. "An emergency notice to Airmen from 20:00 to 20:30 hours has been imposed, the RAF are suspending flights on and off except for operational emergencies, when I would suspend the operation, the standby section has been called out, and they have established a cordon at 800 metres." He had pushed them back from the original 300 for their own safety.

Nearer to him, sheltering behind a sand-dune at 250 metres was his close support team, consisting of his Sergeant Major and a Corporal. Like individual members of the cordon they carried two-way radios, and they had also brought a portable electric generator. They had run out a cable from their hideaway to the site of the bomb, to provide power for the electrically fired cartridges of a rocket wrench.

By clamping the jaws of the wrench on to the protruding lip of the pistol it was possible, with the help of cartridge power, to get sufficient torque to start spinning the pistol out on its thread. Indeed, the entire extraction could be achieved in this way by remote control, in perfect safety for the operator. But the sudden and violent withdrawal of the pin from the detonator by mechanical means carried the added danger of an explosion through vibration or friction.

A turn with some sort of wrench, however, was needed to loosen the pistol to the point where it was no more than finger tight. He decided to use an ordinary Stilson wrench, the sort of thing plumbers tightened or loosened pipes with. He had one in his toolkit. It could still agitate the bomb's mechanism, but it was a chance he just had to take. Once he got the pistol loosened, however, he intended to unscrew it by hand.

As he unscrewed it he would be easing the pin back from the detonator, and the lightest of touches was called for. His fingers would be infinitely more sensitive than the jaws of the wrench.

For the record he justified his actions on tape. "I have the rocket wrench on site, but I'm going to use the Stilson. There's no doubt that the fuze is a 78 pistol, and that it is armed."

He continued his recapitulation into the microphone. "The proximity of the bomb to parked aircraft, the transport Hercules, the interceptor Phantoms, the helicopters, and the bomb dump, also the tented domestic camp on the airfield, makes it imperative that the bomb is not detonated, either by accidental or deliberate means. Therefore I intend to extract the pistol (there was a perceptible pause) by hand.

"Before doing this I will place the tape recorder 50 metres from this site." Useless to record his actions and then leave the tape in the total destruction area. He walked over to the nearest hillock and placed the recorder in its box behind it. The microphone lead, previously checked, was just long enough.

"It is now 19:55 hours. The cordon is set. An all-stations radio check has been answered. The sun is receding and a bank of fog is sweeping in from the sea but the cordon is extensive, and I've decided that the weather conditions will not influence the operation, due to start in five minutes."

Even in poor visibility he didn't think anyone could slip through the cordon unnoticed.

It was time to call the control tower on his radio. "Hello Zero, this is One-Niner. Over."

"Zero, send, over." He knew a moment's envy of the snugness of the chap in the control tower.

"One-Niner – I have had a good examination of the pistol, it appears to be in fairly good condition. The locking tab washer appears to be reasonably free. Roger so far, over."

"Zero, Roger, over."

The two locking tabs, one on either side of the pistol, slotted into incisions at the base of the casing. His first task would be to bend them upwards and outwards to unlock the pistol.

"One-Niner. I will not be in contact with you for the next fifteen minutes. Over."

"Zero, Roger, out."

The preparations were over. He was where he had always known he would be, alone with the bomb. He took off his combat jacket and laid it on the ground by the bomb. One by one he placed the tools he needed on the jacket, to protect them from sand. Then he switched on the microphone leading to the tape recorder and resumed the recording.

"I'm now at the bomb." He was kneeling beside it, fidgeting for the most comfortable position. "I'm going to ease off firstly my beret, and then the spring tab locking washers."

The tape recorder continued running as he worked. Presently his voice interrupted the mush hiss of the live tape.

"This is done." He had unlocked the pistol. Picking up the Stilson wrench, he opened its jaws by turning the gnarled nut before clamping it round the lip of the pistol.

"I'm now going to...ease off...the pistol...very, very gently... very, very gently...ease it back off." He tried to be gentle, but it was no good being tentative. The grip had to be firm, and he turned the wrench, the pressure he had to avert was extreme. A pulse in his temple was beating.

"It's beginning to move." It was the most nail-biting moment so far. "It's beginning to move nicely."

He had slacked it off, and that was enough. It would have to be. The wrench was a clumsy tool for so delicate a task. It was an immense relief to get to work with his hands.

The tape of the recorder was still running, but there was a long silence before he spoke again.

"It's moving well…"

There was something reassuring about finger-tip touch. He knew, as he worked, that these moments were crucial, but his hand on the pistol was steady.

It was not that he didn't know fear. Only an idiot could fail to be frightened at the thought of an unexploded bomb with an armed pistol. But he had developed a frame of mind, over the years, which somehow dropped a shutter on all negative thoughts and concentrated with tunnel-like single mindedness on the task. It left him with no spare energy for nervous twitches.

It was fully a quarter of a minute before he spoke again, and then in a flat, unemotional tone, he reported his first setback. "Stop…little bit of a hang up." The pistol had jammed.

It was a climactic moment. What could have caused it? Was this what had happened before? "Perhaps…perhaps it's sand in the thread…H'm."

Indecision, he knew, was his enemy, yet he needed time, time to think it out. Yet time was something he didn't have. Half a minute, perhaps, if only to recharge his batteries.

"I will leave it for a moment, and rest."

If each intake and exhalation of breath became slightly more regular, slightly more controlled, it was an involuntary reaction to tension. If he was heating, it was the warmth of the evening. He could think of no logical cause for the hang up, and no excuse to wait any longer. Further delay might only exacerbate the dangers.

"I'm going to apply some more pressure…" The next ten seconds seemed longer than any countdown. "It's moving… it's moving gently…here we go again…here we go again…" For each successive quarter turn, still intent on preserving the exact sequence for posterity in case of disaster, he repeated the phrase.

"Here we go again…nice and easy…nice and easy…" And then, quietest of all, so that it was almost a whisper, "And here we have…one pistol."

For a sensual moment he savoured its weight in his hand. But relaxation, he knew, could be fatal. No exhilaration yet. The trickiest job was still to be done.

"The pistol is out. I've now to extract the detonator."

Probing for the detonator, with workshop made extractors that kept slipping, caused him the most acute trepidation so far. "These extractors are not really meant for the job." He was talking to himself, puzzling how to find a safer, more efficient way. "H'm. I'm going to try…a set of callipers…and open them out…and see if I can extract the detonator that way."

He picked up the callipers and bent them outwards, judging the spread that was needed, and tried inserting them. They fitted exactly, and he felt them grip. Gingerly now, he eased the detonator towards him. Slowly and smoothly, it came.

"The detonator's out. The job is finished." It had taken him eighteen minutes, three minutes longer than he had forecast in his last call to control. His tone was unbelievably laconic. "Home, bath and bed."

◈ ◈ ◈

If Ralph were to edit his piece today he might add that, unknown to me, this would be the last thing I would ever defuse.

Forty

THE NEXT day the bomb was taken to an area where it would be safe to detonate it and I decided to use it to show the section the new technique of low order detonation. This consisted of using a small, shaped charge containing 30 grams of explosive, mounted on three legs, and placed at a predetermined height above the target. When fired the explosive causes the cone inside the charge to collapse into a red hot metal slug which then instantaneously penetrates the bomb casing causing the explosive in the bomb to ignite, the pressure from this causing the bomb casing to split open, all in a matter of seconds. My demonstration of the technique went well and the bomb was made safe in seconds. I received a letter from the Commanding Officer of the Falklands conflict.

My dear Steve,

I was aware that a British Mk13 bomb had been located at RAF Stanley on the afternoon of 29 December and that you personally successfully defused it later that evening. What I was not aware of, until my attention was drawn to the brief report you wrote after the incident, was that to diffuze this bomb you extracted the detonator by hand rather than by using a ballistic torque wrench which I understand to be the normal technique.

I applaud your decision to do this – your appreciation of the other constraining factors was excellent – and I offer my congratulations to you for a difficult and dangerous job carried out with courage and skill. Well done.

Yours sincerely,
David Thorne Major General,
DC Thorne CBE

❖ ❖ ❖

The Prime Minister, Margaret Thatcher and her husband Dennis visited the Falkland Islands and during the visit they came to where we were clearing ordnance, and having been introduced, Mrs Thatcher asked about the work and expressed gratitude for what we were doing. Dennis Thatcher asked me about the undetectable mines and started to suggest means of dealing with the problem when the Prime Minister, who, with her entourage, was moving on, said "Come along ,Dennis, I am sure that Major Hambrook knows what he is doing!"

Like most soldiers I took pride in my physical fitness, running each day and enjoying walks of up to 20 miles as a recreation. On January 13, 1983 I ran over Two Sisters Peak to visit the EOD section working there, it was an arduous and enjoyable jog. I returned to my accommodation comfortably tired but pleased with my prowess. The following day I and two others took the Chinook taxi run to Fox Bay West where we were to inspect a minefield fence for damage. All mine clearance had been stopped for some months when it became painfully obvious through mounting casualties, that there was no safe or certain way of either locating or detecting them. Detecting equipments simply had not kept up with the development of plastics made to replace metal. Many of the mines laid possessed the admirable quality of being non-detectable.

On arrival we reported into the command post of the infantry responsible for the defence of the area and got clearance to go to the marked and fenced minefield. We borrowed a vehicle and driver and when we got into walking distance, we dismounted and sent the driver to a point where we would meet him at the end of our walk along the fence.

Crossing the bleak and sparsely grassed terrain toward the clearly visible minefield fence, we passed through a line of standard army iron pickets. Some were partially installed and others were laid on the ground. I drew the guide's attention to them and asked their purpose. He didn't know and assumed that infantry were using the area for training. About 50 metres through the line of pickets and about 70 metres short of the fence, I saw a small crater which was marked by short pickets and white tape. It was instantly identified as a crater left by an exploded anti-personnel mine. Again, I questioned the guide who suddenly remembered that five months before, an islander's Land Rover lost a wheel to a exploding mine which was outside the fenced area. The guide's unit then started to construct a fence at a distance from the mine crater, where it was reasonable to assume there were no more. The fence line had been laid out and erection had just started when they were called away to a higher priority task near Port Stanley. The fence at Fox Bay had not only not been completed but the need to do so was forgotten. This left the three of us in an area thought to contain mines but without any help at hand.

Although I was a Major, the reconnaissance was commanded by the Captain. This was right and proper as he had served with his unit, which had the responsibility for locating and fencing the mine fields in the area, for six months. His local knowledge was greater than mine. However, the danger of the situation led me to take the responsibility to get us safely to the fence where there was a proven safe path along its length.

There were vehicle tracks leading towards the fence, and having told the others to walk two paces behind me and tread where I had trod, we moved slowly toward safety. I have a good eye for the unusual and we made good progress until we came to a strip about four metres wide which the settlement manager had run a cultivator across, hoping to see if there were any more mines! The surface was broken and disturbed and all weathering characteristics that would indicate the position of a mine destroyed. Carefully, I picked my way with the others following as before. I got to the edge of firm ground just four paces away from the safe path, took another step and was thrown forward and down, deafened by an explosion and gripped by intense pain. I realised immediately that I had been injured by an exploding mine. My face was on the ground and from the corner of my eye I could see the shining sun. I knew I could either sit up and get on with living or lie there and die.

Sit up man, and be a man, I thought.

"Keep calm and stay where you are," I shouted to my colleagues. I forced myself upright. My companions had run to the safe path, the incident had shaken them badly but the pain, and my companions' horrified expressions, told me that I had been seriously injured. I could see that my left knee cap was shattered and exposed. I was unable to move my legs so, using my hands I shuffled on my bottom to the other three men. The pain was excruciating but as the others seemed shocked and unable to help me I resolved to remain conscious, come what may. It was fortunate that I could not see the injuries to my lower legs as if I had, like those around me, my strength might have evaporated. I became extremely angered by their reactions. Rebuking one until he calmed from his anxious "I am injured" state – a stone or something had hit him on the back – to one where he would listen, I sent him off along the safe path which ran along the fence line to the vehicle and told him to get help.

I took off my belt and tied it around my left thigh as a tourniquet. Unable to bend my legs, I assumed that my foot had been blown off. I lifted my left leg with both hands and forced it to lie across my right, aiming to get the larger wounds out of the dirt. The remains of the calf length boot on my left leg was swinging about and the pain was excruciating. I gave my jack knife to a colleague and told him to cut the bits of boot off but leave the top in place so that the laces I had tied that morning could be another temporary tourniquet. I then made the only serious mistake since standing on the mine by emptying my standard issue ampoule of morphine into my left leg. It had no effect and probably ran straight out of the blood in the leg's explosively opened end.

As I waited for help, I began to pick pieces of green plastic from my leg. I realised that I'd stood on an Italian anti-personnel mine. Only a small amount of explosive was used but its purpose was to incapacitate someone and cause a drain on the manpower of a unit. The Captain knelt and put his arm around me which was very comforting. As my right thigh was bleeding through my tattered trousers, it seemed a sensible move to cut through them above my knee and apply some first aid. There followed the most disgusting noise I have ever heard – a squishy plop as a lump of detached tissue, blood and muscle fell from within my trousers to the ground. I hastily pressed my beret and remaining trouser material onto the wound, rebound my thigh as tightly as I could, and crudely secured the improvised dressing with my whistle lanyard.

Three Infantry soldiers carrying first aid kits arrived then. They'd been alerted by the soldier I sent to get help, and had run over a mile. They put shell dressings over my wounds to stem the bleeding but kept my tourniquets in place. I was grateful for their presence and efforts and my mind remained clear whilst we awaited help, suffering the mortification of seeing two helicopters circling over a minefield some two miles away. Fortunately I was carrying a small distress flare gun containing six miniature flares. The Captain had fired off five. He was facing away from them and as I could see the helicopters over his shoulder, I told him to wait, then when I saw one of them facing us I told him, "Now." The helicopter saw the flare and came straight to us.

Forty One

ONCE in the helicopter, I was laid behind the pilots' seats on a buoyancy aid. The pilot asked if he should go to Goose Green, which was the nearest medical centre, but I'd seen the Medical Officer leave and get into a Chinook with his fishing gear just before we landed at Fox Bay West. I told the pilot this and we made our way to Port Stanley landing first at Teal Inlet for fuel.

The flight seemed to go on forever but it was probably only an hour long. I was laying on a buoyancy aid and by the time we arrived, I had bitten a hole in it trying to relieve my pain. The helicopter landed in a field fairly close to the hospital where an army ambulance and my personal driver were waiting. What happened next was farcical as the medic looked into the helicopter, then spoke into his radio, "His right foot is missing."

"It's my left," I said."

He then attempted to pull me from the helicopter by my leg. I swore at him and told him to go round the other side and get me out using my shoulders. I was laid on a folding stretcher and carried to the nearby ambulance where the carriers discovered the stretcher was too long and didn't fit. Placing the stretcher on their heads as they made efforts to get it into the ambulance, the sides dropped and I started to slide off.

Just when I thought my troubles were going to include being dropped on my head, my driver rushed across, got hold of the stretcher, held up the side and told the medics to place it on the ambulance floor which they did. It set off, siren blaring, at high speed across the bumpy field until I shouted at them to slow down as the bumping was painful.

The hospital was only a few hundred yards away and once inside, I saw some of my men and my second in command. I asked him if everyone had left the minefield safely and ordered that no message relating to the extent of my injuries be sent to my home until I was properly assessed.

Having felt that it was my duty to stay conscious until I handed over command to him I did so and said, "Right Mike, it's yours. And I'll be needing some crutches." This caused word to go round that Hambrook hadn't changed!

The medical teams together with the surgeons and support units that had been in the Falklands throughout the war, had left, leaving a skeleton medical team behind. The team did not include surgeons and in addition, my family were told that I had lost both legs. The doctor and nurses got to work then, cutting off my uniform and injecting me. I didn't wake up for a day and when I did, I discovered that I had been given a Symes amputation, where the remains of the foot are cut off at the ankle and the heel stitched onto the stump. It got its name from Doctor Symes who practised in Scotland in the 18th century. At the time it was a big step forward as it enabled people to walk on their stump.

Neither the army Medical Officer nor the Falkland Island's civilian doctor, who was Scottish, were surgeons but they did the operation as to delay might have allowed infection and mean I'd have to have more of my leg removed. Even though I'd really lost my foot more than my leg, the Symes caused me considerable problems since a more usual amputation is through the mid-calf which makes the provision of a prosthetic limb much easier.

I have strong faith in prayer and this was reinforced by my experience after I was injured. During my unconsciousness I found myself in a dark passage or corridor being drawn irresistibly toward a partially opened door from which streamed warm and welcoming light and the sounds of happy voices. The compulsion to go through the door was almost overwhelming and I felt myself moving readily toward it. But suddenly I knew that if I did I would not see my children and wife again. I fought savagely against my forward movement and slowly the welcoming door receded and I assume that I slept.

As I woke up, I was told to look down at my amputation. I laughed and said, "Oh, thank you – you've sewn my toes back on." The large stitches made it look that way.

That day, as I regained consciousness, I struggled to come to terms with my situation. I wondered what the future held. I knew my family would love and support me, but I was unsure about my future in the military, which was everything. I also had my concerns about the unusual amputation. But I had to accept what was happening.

Shortly after midday I felt as though I was being wrapped in a warm and protective cocoon. I felt safe and loved. The next week when I was sufficiently well to speak to my wife by radio phone it transpired that the feeling I had experienced of loving and protective safety coincided in real time with the praying by the congregation of our family church for my recovery and safe return home. This reinforced my faith and removed any fear of death.

There were two of us on the ward. The other chap was an RAF Station Commander who was not badly injured. But it was pretty quiet, so I amused myself by listening to Mendelssohn's Death March on a Walkman. It sounds a bit morbid but it was all I had, a friend had lent it to me. It was actually very soothing.

In 1967, when I was the senior military instructor at an army diving school located on a German naval base in Kiel, contact with the forces of other nations was frequent and the universal rapport that exists between divers led to friendly working and social relationships. Often mutual difficulties and similar were discussed between us without any compromise to each others' security rules. During a discussion on the technique of clearing mines that could be laid underwater in the canals and rivers of Europe during any time of conflict, I was shown a Nordic manufacturer's brochure relating to a process whereby fibreglass, plastics and explosives were mixed to produce mines that would be extremely difficult, if not impossible, to detect. As the mines were in production this seemed to be an important development in the field of mine warfare especially as mines invariably require to be detected and removed.

I wrote a short paper based on the products, their threat and the difficulties that would arise from attempting to detect and clear such mines using the standard service mine detector. Clearly, the time had come for research into the subject and the development of an instrument to allow the safe and efficient clearance of the nefarious items. The paper, complete with the brochures obtained through the good services of a personal friend, was sent to the Corps Headquarters BAOR. After a period of time I received acknowledgement of its receipt and was also informed that the Commander regarded it to be of importance. As such it had been forwarded to the appropriate authority in the UK for consideration. One does not have to be clairvoyant to understand my feelings when, serving in the Falklands some 16 years later on, I lost a foot and sustained other injuries in the explosion of a plastic mine that could not be detected by the still current, circa 1967, mine detector!

Within three days of the incident I received a personal letter from the Prime Minister expressing her distress and regret at my injuries and sending me good wishes for the future.

I spent two weeks in the hospital receiving good treatment and learning how to use crutches, then I was flown back to England. It was a long and painful flight on a stretcher aboard a Hercules troop carrier to Ascension Island and from there to RAF Brize Norton on a VC10, where I did at least have a seat. I spent the journey consoling a soldier who had broken his leg and was in absolute agony, telling him about some ridiculous press coverage I'd had before my injury.

A reporter from the News of the World who'd been in the Falklands said to me, "A king penguin's been blown up, what do you think of that?"

"Better a penguin than a soldier," I replied.

I don't like to see anything get blown up and I love animals. I literally meant rather a penguin than someone's husband, brother or father. They printed my comment and I got hate mail. Extraordinary.

In true army style I was lifted in and out of the Hercules by forklift, a height of about 17 feet. After the plane landed in the UK we were transferred to an RAF coach where I was put, once again on a stretcher, on the floor of the aisle. A very bumpy ride followed

– it felt as though the driver relished hitting traffic bumps at speed and I was desperate to get home. On arrival at the RAF hospital I was delighted to be greeted by my wife and children who had been driven there by my Commanding Officer. He and I spoke briefly then he discreetly left me with my family. They told me they had been dancing about when they heard I'd lost a leg as they were originally told I had lost both. We spoke of my wounds and I drew back the bed sheet to show them that it was really only a foot missing and that the minor injuries to both legs would soon heal. Whilst I was doing this the ward sister came in and was horrified at what I was doing until my wife explained why.

Two days later I was transferred to the Queen Elizabeth Military Hospital at Woolwich. It was a fairly long journey, much of it along motorways, and I was very bored since the civilian driver and two nurses sat in the front chatting as though I wasn't there. This was compounded when the ambulance pulled into a service station and the trio bid me farewell with a cheerful, "We won't be long," and went for refreshments. I lay there mentally tasting the warm drink to come but alas on their return there was nothing for me and I was relieved when we reached the hospital and I was returned to army hands.

"I have never seen one like that. You'll have to have more cut off."

The physiotherapist's words were not a cheering welcome. But apart from him, the care was excellent. I was told that the stitches would be removed on Friday and when Friday morning came, with the physiotherapist's words ringing in my ears, I refused the usual sedative so that I could hear what the surgeons were saying.

The removal of the stitches was painful and I was quite tense. But when the surgeon said, "You have a healthy stump," I was so pleased that I asked him to repeat it. He did and then I was able to relax. The sister took me to the recovery ward but the surgeon said it was unnecessary as I'd not been sedated and I was told that I could go home that afternoon. My unit was informed and a car sent but before I was cleared to leave, I had to prove my ability to use crutches by going down a flight of stairs to the ground floor, which I did – nothing was going to stop me going home. A wheelchair was in the main entrance for me to collect but when the car arrived and the driver came to me, I got up onto my crutches and asked him to wheel the chair outside. Then, with some difficulty, I got into the car and told my driver to leave the wheelchair where it was. I was driven home to be met by my wife and our children.

Gill had paid me a great compliment when I was injured. A Commander wrote to her expressing his sympathy and she replied, "If it had to happen to someone, better it is Stephen because I know he is strong enough to overcome it."

Understandably, my mother was very upset by my injury, my father too. He came to visit me in hospital. I had a lot of scabs on my remaining leg and because of that I couldn't bear to have the covers on me. His face when he saw me told me how he felt and he gave me a hug.

Forty Two

BACK in Sittingbourne, I started getting my life back together. Every day, regardless of the weather, I went out on my crutches, increasing the distance I covered every time. I took delivery of an automatic car which needed no adapting since I could manage the controls with my right foot. Having been advised to apply for a Blue Badge giving me more freedom in parking, we went to the local Social Services office to enquire. I was told by the receptionist that the office I required was upstairs and there was no lift. I lifted my injured leg and put the stump onto her desk. No further words were needed and the staff came down to me.

Six months after I was injured, I passed the army's strenuous annual Basic Fitness Test and my diving medical and returned to duty. Given my rank, I was always destined for a desk job after the Falklands, so there was no psychological adjustment for me to make there, and having obtained the car but lacking a leg, I returned to my desk and my role as Quartermaster. This involved a lot of organising, phone calls, list making, ordering and preparing. My comrades and the Officer Commanding were supportive of my rehabilitation so my time was split about 50/50 between that and my work. I returned to the Queen Elizabeth hospital for some necessary but gruelling rehabilitation. One exercise was so intense that I hated it to the point of fear. Tweaking, it was called. First, I had to have ice packs placed on my rigid left knee, replenished as they defrosted, for about half an hour. This caused intense discomfort as did even minimal changes of temperature whilst the wounds were still settling. When the physiotherapist, a large and burly Australian, judged my knee to be sufficiently numb with the cold I would be turned onto my stomach and invited to grit my teeth, or scream, whichever was best, whilst he used his considerable strength and weight to make the knee bend a little more. I am not ashamed to say that I cried with pain and dreaded the cheerful cry of, "Just one more," and "Let's find another degree of bend." I arrived at the hospital with a stiff leg and by the time I left, it had improved to a bend of 15 degrees.

To avoid a permanently stiff leg and not wishing to drive a round trip of 112 miles once or twice a week I devised two exercises that I could do at home. No less painful but my groans and tears would at least be in the family. The first involved a length of rope to which a strap was joined by a large and very strong spring. I sat on the dining table with its edge behind my knees. My wife would pass the rope under the table and fasten the strap around my stump. The other end of the rope was passed over my shoulder into my hands. When I felt sufficiently brave I would pull hard on the rope forcing my leg to bend around and under the table edge, my pulling stretched the spring and the resulting tension kept a pull on my stiff joint in-between the more violent movements.

The second exercise was equally simple. We bought an exercise bicycle and set the saddle lower than it would normally have been for me. My stump was strapped to the one pedal and I would pedal with my good leg, the fixed wheel action of the cycle forcing my stiff leg and body up whilst my weight upon the low saddle pushed against the lifting movement. It was crude, painful, but very effective and within three months I had regained full flexibility of the knee. Although there was no kneecap and some damage to the joint, over time my exercising caused a ligament and cartilage to form to replace it.

Pain often came upon me suddenly and without warning and when it did, I would be compelled to instantly stop what I was doing or saying until the moment had passed. We coped as a family by deciding that I would be left to overcome the twinge without comment and then we would take up the activity or conversation as though the moment had never been. A source of strength and great comfort was the way my wife and children on seeing tears on my face would just reach out, gently grip my arm or shoulder and without a word go on with what they were doing.

Even achieving small things myself gave me a sense that I was getting there. One day when I was alone in the house I wanted a cup of tea. I got onto my crutches to fill and put the kettle on while leaning against the kitchen unit. I made the tea then, as the dining table was some way away, I carefully put the mug on the floor, got down myself and holding the mug, I gently shuffled on my bottom across the floor to the table where I reached up and put the mug on the table. Then I lifted myself up and onto a dining chair. Never had tea tasted sweeter!

One day in the office I heard my own voice. I went to investigate and found staff sorting items returned to the unit from the Falkland Islands. They had found the tape I had made whilst dealing with the bomb on Port Stanley airfield and were enjoying listening to it. I let them finish listening and then claimed the tape as my own. I still have it.

I attended a local disability centre to start the process of obtaining a prosthetic limb. I was accepted as a patient but I intensely disliked being spoken about and discussed over my head as though I wasn't there. I was also asked when I had the motorcycle accident that had caused my disability. I asked to see my file and discovered that it was the wrong one.

As a war veteran, I was able to choose where I could get medical help. So, disillusioned, I transferred to the Roehampton disability centre. There was my first indication of the difficulty I would experience in getting treatment for a Symes amputation. I was fitted with a stump sheath made of leather with steel support rods connected to a can-shaped walking surface which had to do for two months. When I returned home it was immediately christened Dad's hoof especially as the portion visible below my trouser leg bottom resembled an animal's foot. It was painful to wear because the leather chafed but at least I was reasonably mobile again and could get around at work without crutches.

The hoof was supposed to be worn for two months but it was three months later that I got a reasonably fitting fibre glass limb. It was rigid as there was not sufficient room between the end of my stump and the fitted foot to allow a flexible joint. Despite this I began a daily 10 mile course at a training circuit near my office. It took me a couple of hours but it made me much stronger and I was soon able to partially run, although doing this I found it necessary to change the woollen stump socks worn inside the limb to avoid blistering of my stump.

Quite soon after I came home from the Falklands, I joined the British Limbless Ex-Service Men's Association (BLESMA) and later that year Gill and I were invited to Twin Peaks in Colorado. I was to enjoy some rehabilitative skiing and she could relax and visit local attractions. We flew into Canada with the RAF, then British Airways flew us for free to Washington where we had dinner as guests of the American Veterans Agency before we flew on to Colorado. It was enjoyable, as was the skiing, which I found reasonably easy once I had got used to the ski lift.

I remain a member of BLESMA to this day and over the years would become a branch welfare officer and chairman of the South East England Area Committee. In the early days, I was given help and advice regarding my position and the provision of limbs and any relevant allowances. I also met the only other serviceman I know to have a Symes amputation, a young Marine Captain who told me about a Canadian, Professor Davies, who had an experimental limb-making unit at Roehampton. I contacted Professor Davies and was invited to participate in his programme. He used a computerised milling machine to make a cast from exact measurements taken from the patient. As opposed to being one of many seen in one day by the NHS, with Professor Davies a whole day was designated to each person. It was a highly individual treatment whereas at one of my NHS appointments my limb was taken for the whole day and I was forgotten until the clinic closed. I don't think I was very popular with the NHS doctors for going to him, but there we are.

A few months after my fibreglass limb, Professor Davis produced a leg for me, my third, and I was helped to put it on. He asked me to walk along his catwalk. I did and quite naturally at the end I turned to walk back, turning normally towards my left foot, where previously I had turned to the right lifting my left leg round with me. When I got home, the children were playing in the garden so I went out to see them and climbed a ladder that was leaning against a wall. They were so excited that Daddy had a proper foot!

After Professor Davis returned to Canada, I heard about a centre at Birmingham doing similar work so I drove there and they accepted me as a patient. I needed adaptations because the muscle was wasting away and my leg was getting smaller. It is now only the width of a lady's forearm. They produced me a new limb.

Eight years ago I decided to go private. I knew Dorset Orthopaedic through BLESMA. I stayed in a guest house close to their site. They made me a prototype leg. I'd go off and walk two or three miles, come back and tell them what needed changing. I came back once with the foot back to front where it had slipped round. I stayed a week and by the end I had a leg that I could walk on. I tested it round the New Forest, round the Rufus Stone, and the local area. I could play an 18-hole golf round. Very few people were even aware that I had an artificial leg. I have even been able to dive with it.

Originally though, I did have to use the NHS for my prosthetic. One doctor I saw took one look at my leg and said, "It's all skin and bone."

It was surprising how many people said thoughtless things and I am fortunate that I am made of strong stuff because that could really have affected some people to hear that.

In 2003, Dr Andrew Murrison, the then shadow minister for health (with an active interest in defence policy), did a review of the experience of Falklands veterans. He visited disability centres and what he found was appalling – poorly ordered stock including one place where there were 200 wheelchairs that were useless due to being the wrong size. Esther Rantzen did a programme on the issue, using my leg.

The finished report seemed to be taking a very long time to be produced so I wrote to Margaret Thatcher and said that many of us had co-operated and was there now some reluctance to publish? The report was published a few days later.

Forty Three

I N DECEMBER 1983, less than a year after my injury in the
January of that year, I joined the Regimental Marching Team
to participate in the East Kent Half Marathon, raising money
for Canterbury Pilgrim's Hospice. This really encouraged me in
my fitness as I had to nag some of the others to keep up with me.
This was in preparation for the 25-Mile Chichester March taking
place on August 25, 1984 – an annual event organised by the Royal
Military Police.

The march went well and as a team we supported each other so
that we finished as we started, a tired but elated regimental team. I
raised £4,000 for RADAR – the Royal Association for Disability and
Rehabilitation, now the Royal Association for Disability Rights –
which I was delighted about.

A reception by the lord mayor of Chichester followed and as
well as the certificate we each received, I was awarded a plate trophy
for being the most deserving and inspirational marcher of the day.
I regarded this as a great honour and it sits on the wall of my study
along with other items I prize.

In 1989, the regiment decided to enter the Chichester March.
I wanted to be part of the team but the Warrant Officer who was
forming and training the team told me I was too old. This rankled
so I entered the march as an individual and did my own training,
marching 27 miles twice a week.

It was hard but I was determined to avenge what I considered to
be an insult.

Four months later the day arrived and I was up at 5am to get myself and my marching equipment in order. I ate breakfast, collected my bits and strolled to the start looking the height of fashion in army boots, blue shorts, t-shirt and an old jungle hat. I made last minute adjustments to the distribution of the 13kgs of necessary items I had hung about my body – including spare leg – while discreetly shuffling and elbowing into a favourable position. Seven thirty am arrived and away we went. The swift of foot were well away, leading the field into a tight right turn and a mighty cheer went up when it became clear that the sprinters had turned right instead of left and found themselves in a car park. Great fun for those of us at the rear.

The course quickly led into a very narrow and deeply rutted track along which we all jostled to pass quickly. The unscrupulous used elbows freely to force a passage through the throng, my elbows were quite sore. Out of the lane and on the road leading to the South Downs, the pace was good and I strode along as best I could. Some distance out my stump signalled it was time for a sock change. I dropped to my bottom, took my limb off, wiped my stump, put a dry sock and my limb back on and I was up and away. Practise brought the time for a sock change down to less than a minute. My first stop invoked friendly enquiries from fellow marchers and an anxious policeman on a motorbike. He would reappear at intervals throughout the following five hours with the same concern. There's always one clever fellow and during one change a team went by and someone made a sarcastic remark about spare legs.

"I'd rather have my leg than your mouth," I retorted, earning a cheer from those in earshot.

At checkpoint one, the scramble to get drinking water was daunting. I had a full water bottle on my belt and decided not to stop. Stump sock changes became necessary with annoying regularity. There was a simple equation to it – when ache becomes agony, stop. This was irritating as those I had passed whilst moving caught up with me while I was sat on my bottom. In 25 miles I changed my sock 13 times. By checkpoint two, the sun was blazing from a clear sky and the field was thinning noticeably, the runners had long gone but the 4mph marchers were in the lead and I was among them. My wish to finish hardened into a calculating determination to beat anyone I could. Stops became slicker, drink and food were consumed on the move, rest stops were ignored and my prancing boots saw me flying along the endless rutted and flint strewn tracks.

A little way after checkpoint three, I gave my plasters and sweets to a lad in sore need of them. I decided to reward myself with a muesli bar and was horrified to find it had fallen from an unfastened pouch. Those following probably credited the organisers with laying a treasure trail. At checkpoint four, temptingly located next to an open pub (which I passed with averted eyes), I moved into the long grind back to Goodwood and those marching a shorter route joined in. I stopped to give water and help to a distressed young lady and fortunately my solicitous policeman appeared, enabling me to continue. Getting back into my stride was hard and approaching Goodwood race course others suddenly streamed passed. This was demoralising until I realised these were the fresh, shorter distance starters.

At Goodwood the route turned left, straight up and over the heights. I found this very difficult and physically sickening as the heat was now intense and checkpoint five and water was some distance away. If during the climb I had been offered an ice cream I would have sat down and not moved for a week. Once over the broad crest I tried hard to regain control of mind and body. I hit a steep descent into a valley immediately followed by a precipitous ascent back over the Downs. This took some hacking. I spoke to my short leg, it screamed back and together we scrambled to the top, crying, cursing and crawling but we made it to a beautiful view. About five miles away was Chichester Cathedral, seemingly all downhill or flat.

Oh deceitful eye – the route led into a narrow and heavily rutted lane with high banks. It was very hot, very dusty and extremely difficult with so many large flints laying loose that it was like scrambling through shale. How I blessed my army boots and felt for those wearing trainers. The jumble of humanity in the lane was very dense but my pride and boots were now beyond control and dragged me on. Crying out, "Look out, my leg is running away with me," created gaps through which I slipped and moved on. Age must have mellowed me because when I was younger I would have tripped up those in front and run over them.

Through checkpoint five and on to a firmer surface for the final miles, once more I caught a team which I had already passed seven times before losing my advantage to a vital stump stop. A quick mental battle followed during which my mind downgraded vital to necessary and then unnecessary. I would ignore the pain and not stop again, I wanted to beat them back, take off my limb and sooth my parboiled and sore stump.

With the finish in sight, a cry of "Hi, Dad!" urged me on. The unexpected encouragement from my daughters was very moving and I crossed the finish line with misty eyes and a finish time of five hours and 52 minutes, an average speed of just over 4.5mph. I sat near the finish line with a drink in my hand and waited half an hour for the regimental team. Honour satisfied, I bought them all a beer.

During the march a number of us had passed and repassed each other and generally moved along as a peer group. After finishing, some of them thanked me explaining that the sight of my white plastic leg passing yet again made them determined to finish. This, together with my daughters' pride, was the most satisfying compliment I have ever received. Perhaps now I will share the secret of my unrestrained gallop – a pair of restless boots and a Walkman with a tape of cavalry marches – my thinking being that if they can urge those with four legs, how much more would they do for one and a half!

Sometime before the march I had been to hospital for an arthroscopy, an operation on both knees relating to my strenuous lifestyle not my amputation. Since the issue was wear and tear, a nursing sister and I disagreed about the amount of walking I should be doing. I asked her why since, following the surgery, I had progressed from using crutches to an occasional walking stick, she now wanted to halt my progress. I needed to exercise my partial return to normality, she responded by taking the stick away. We were obviously both strong characters but I felt that my need to enjoy escaping my crutches was more important to me than her need to exercise authority over a short stay patient. We discussed the matter firstly somewhat emotionally and then in a rational manner.

"You are bloody minded," she said.

"No I am not, I am determined," I replied.

I got my stick back when I agreed the compromise of being "bloody determined." And bless her, if she didn't appear at each of the Chichester checkpoints to remind me that being "bloody determined" would ensure I finished.

We raised a reasonable sum of money for our regimental charity, SIN (Soldiers In Need) and additionally I raised funds for the church of St Thomas in Canterbury which had suffered considerable damage in the Great Storm of 1987, and once again the Canterbury Pilgrim's Hospice. When it opened in 1973, my wife was the volunteer secretary. The building had been used as a kitchen by the King's School, Canterbury, so I took a fortnight's leave and went to clear grease from the drains and other things. Whenever the hospice had open days, The Queen lent them her marquees. Not that she knew about it. I didn't think she would mind as long as I returned them to our barracks.

That afternoon we gathered in Chichester town hall to be given our certificates and medals. Once again I had proved that being disabled was not the end to life.

Forty Four

IN MIDDLE of 1983, Gill and I decided to sell our individual homes and buy something that would suit us as the years went on. We wanted something that was within commuting distance of my unit but away from the military environment. We looked at a number of properties but the one we chose was in a village called Tyler Hill, in Kent. Built in about 1830 as two cottages, it had at some time been converted into one house and stands in a hedged plot of about a third of an acre. It has such a lovely, homely feel and remains my home today.

Having secured the house there were alterations needed but before we did them we went to Australia for six weeks to visit my wife's relations. Arriving in Melbourne, the first thing I did was the Melbourne Marathon, a reporter and Gill's relatives having found donors. It came about after an Australian reporter had seen me doing the 10 mile marathon. We'd got chatting, I told him we were off to Australia and he invited me to participate. I literally got off the plane, into a car to the start line and raced!

We hired a car from a firm known as Rent-a-Wreck – a massive old Ford with a boot large enough for the children to sleep in – and made our way to the Rainforest. Having driven from Melbourne, we moved onto a township named Traralgon in Victoria. We explored the surrounding area then went into a bush shack in Birregurra where the only other dwelling was a rundown garage and shop about three miles away. There we spent 10 days pulling our own water, cutting logs for the fire and living a basic but enjoyable life. We also visited my brother-in-law and his wife in Sale and enjoyed a folk song evening with them. They told us that an Englishman called Johnny often sang and when he came in, I saw that it my cousin Johnny Brown – what an extraordinarily small world it is. We had a great evening.

Soon it was time to return to the UK and our new home but until we got to the airport we didn't know Australia won't let you leave with too much of their currency. We quickly looked for a bank into which to pay our surplus and I decided to buy a bottle of whisky to bring back tax free. I nursed its passage home then found that a larger bottle in the local supermarket was cheaper.

Leaving Sittingbourne meant that the girls had to leave their convent school. I asked them if there was anything they wished to do to celebrate and they were unanimous – they wanted to burn the brown knickers they'd had to wear. A line of sticks went up in the back garden, the knickers were hung on them and with the help of some fuel ceremoniously burnt. My wife and I agreed that they did indeed look very uncomfortable things to wear. The children were placed in St. Thomas' primary school in Canterbury, travelling daily on the school minibus. It was a good school and they enjoyed being in a class with Gill's son, Morris.

The garden's vegetable patch had raised brick retaining walls with square corners. I took the top three layers off to lower the walls and a good friend curved the square corners. Having decided to have part of the planned lawn about eight inches above the main lawn, he then built an attractive curved retaining wall across the area which also contained three fruit trees. I made enquiries about obtaining top soil to level the patch and to fill the raised area and to our delight a local farmer arrived un-asked with a trailer full of good soil. He helped to wheelbarrow it into place and then refused payment. We were very grateful.

We started work on the actual house then. We also commissioned a local architect to draw up plans for a typical Kentish half-hipped roof over the lounge which was a flat-roofed extension, and a period-style porch. In the lounge we had a farmhouse fireplace constructed of old Kentish bricks. In the kitchen we replaced the plastic tiles with quarry tiles. Our plastic units were taken out and given to a local policeman. We decided to have the free standing heating boiler in the kitchen moved to a more convenient position. The heating engineer required the mains water supply into the house turned off at the main stopcock but we had no idea where the main stopcock was. Out with the divining rods I went, accompanied by the children who were armed with twigs to use as markers. I criss-crossed the front garden until I got a reaction, then a second reaction gave me a line to work along and the children busily pegged it. Having got to a rockery close to the boundary hedge I located the stopcock buried within it so I cleared the soil and growth and was able to use the key to turn it off. I ensured that it wasn't buried again and later had a meter installed which reduced the water and sewerage charges considerably. When news of my ability to find water pipes got around the village I was asked regularly to help others by doing the same for them.

I certainly developed a hyper awareness as a result of my job. You might say that I would get feelings about things. Once in Northern Ireland I was going down into a cellar and I got a feeling something was wrong. It turned out that there was a trip switch wired to an explosive charge on the third step down. My in-laws at the time challenged me on these skills. They asked me to go out of the room and they hid something. I was to guess what and where. As I waited to be allowed back into the room I saw in my mind's eye my relations hiding a piece of silver under the carpet. I went into the room and identified what they had done immediately. There was a saying in the unit, "Hambrook can smell 'em, it's in his water." But really it was a keen sense of observation and the ability to think through the logic that would have been employed by whoever laid the mine.

I converted the double garage into a workshop and started to build oak and pine units in the utility room. It was hard work but fortunately the experience I acquired renovating my previous home stood me in good stead. I worked most evenings until late and at the weekends making steady progress – although we were without a usable kitchen for nearly two years. My wife was a talented seamstress and made the curtains for eight rooms and lined bamboo blinds for the kitchen and utility room. We scoured secondhand shops and antique sellers looking for old pine furniture and when the half-hipped roof was built we had a floor put in and I created a hobby room complete with workbench and power sockets, which the children used as they wished.

The girls started to learn to use computers at school. Not having one myself and unable to answer their questions, I bought an Amstrad desktop and quickly became reasonably proficient. I enjoyed this and bought another computer for my office at work. Together with a former army colleague, I took courses in various computing skills including one at the University of Kent and my personal proficiently increased to a level where I was able to teach others.

My wife had a hard-to-control type 2 diabetes called brittle diabetes and she relied on daily insulin injections. This was a condition that I learned to manage and I would help her if she had an insulin reaction. I hoped that her condition would not deteriorate with time as my love for her was intense. One of her symptoms was that she would appear quite normal but her mind would wander, a sort of dementia and she could become quite spiteful and emotional. She would collapse sometimes too. She became a patient of a specialist consultant at the military hospital in Woolwich who admitted her to the hospital as an in-patient where she stayed for 10 months with no apparent success.

Forty Five

MY voluntary BLESMA duties involved visiting servicemen and their widows across Kent to ensure they were receiving all they were entitled to and to help them resolve any problems. The regiment supported this activity. I also visited new amputees in Woolwich military hospital. There was no system in place for this to happen otherwise, which was a surprise. The support given from places like Headley Court today are as a result of recent conflicts.

One young man had been riding his motorcycle when the car in front of him stopped and the driver opened his door. This caught the youngster on the motorcycle and ripped his left leg off. By a stroke of almost unbelievable luck the car behind contained four doctors who gave lifesaving first aid until the ambulance arrived. After some months he was fit enough to go to his home, which was near Gilwern in Wales.

When I went to see him, he didn't notice that I was also an amputee and that was important – that they could see how normal my life was, and then they found out. As I had got to know him I was asked by BLESMA if I would take him home in my car. Accompanied by Gill, we made our way and arrived at his home, which was a smallholding, to be greeted by his delighted parents, after which the lad went around the patch using his crutches and feeling his way back into the homely atmosphere. This was a pleasure to see. After chatting to his parents we made our way to the nearby pub where we were booked in for the night.

The next morning after breakfast we returned to see how the lad was doing and found him riding side saddle on a small motorbike. We had decided to visit the Brecon Beacons National Park. It was a fantastic drive along very narrow tracks which ran high around a lake then made a precipitous descent to a B road, following which we made the long drive back to Kent.

I still had my motor cycle but because the gear lever was operated by the left foot this made it difficult for me to ride safely. Having spoken to the unit fitter, he suggested a bracket that would be bolted onto the gear lever and extend about two inches above it. This would allow me to either put my foot under it and lift up or onto it, and push down depending on which gear it was in. Once fitted I found this easy and safe to use and I returned to commuting by motor cycle.

Several years later I was riding to work when I pushed down to change gear and the bolt holding my foot to the limb socket broke and my foot dropped off. I then had to leave the bike and hop back about 40 yards looking for a boot with my foot in it. When I found it I remounted and, with the motor cycle in low gear, slowly motored the 15 or so miles back to my home where I had a spare limb. As the outcome of the incident could easily have been more serious I decided that my biking days were over and reluctantly got rid of the machine.

At this time my wife's condition worsened dramatically. She was discharged from Woolwich and I was told by the specialist that her condition was likely to worsen, especially if she had to accept responsibility for others. Sadly, this did happen and my wife became obsessed with upsetting thoughts that if anything happened to me she would become the main family figure. This was distressing for all of us. She also resented my BLESMA responsibilities which I could not abandon. Ultimately it reached the level where she could not accept the responsibility of being a wife or mother and she left. In time we agreed to separate and I helped her to buy a house near her sister while the children, including Morris, remained with me. My wife told a friend that it was best for Morris and that I would be a good father. When Morris was 11 she persuaded him to go and live with his biological father. The girls and I were extremely upset but it was ratified in court and I got access, which I thought was very wise of the judge. Some years later Gill died in a domestic accident, a tragic loss of a wonderful woman.

In 1987 I was awarded a BLESMA National Award, the Frankland Moore Rose Bowl, for my efforts on behalf of the members and widows. This was to be presented at the annual general meeting, which that year was being held in the Metropole Hotel in Brighton – the town where my mother and brothers lived. It was lavish accommodation and the dinner was in the Grand Ballroom. Whilst being served I was surprised to recognise one of the waitresses as my son Stephen's wife who was equally surprised as I had not told my wider family about the event. She gave me a kiss which caused a buzz of excitement especially as I said later that I thought it was part of the award.

One of the things I witnessed during my work with BLESMA has stayed with me. I was visiting a casualty from Northern Ireland. The man had lost both legs and had severe burns to his face. When his wife came to visit him she came into the ward, walked straight over, bent down and kissed his burned lips. I shall never forget that act of supreme devotion.

BLESMA always has a strong presence at Remembrance in London and I have been going since 1984. It's a nice reunion for the members as we gather at a hotel close to Heathrow on the Saturday night before, have dinner and retire to the bar to drink and chat into the night. The following morning it's early breakfast and onto a coach at 8am. The coach reaches Horse Guards Parade ground at about 9.30am and parks in the Mall where a truck loaded with electric buggies is waiting for our arrival. The contingent consists of those able to march around the circular course and those, like myself, who have restricted mobility and require a buggy – defined as walking and non-walking members.

Having been mounted and the order of march established, we all proceed the short distance onto the parade ground which is a melee of young and old men and women, most proudly wearing their medals or those of a member of their family – their own on the left breast and the others on the right breast. The number is more than 1,000 veterans, all greeting former comrades and slowly joining the column in which they will march. It seems like bedlam but when the military band by the Cenotaph starts to play, it is amazing to see everybody straighten up, ready to march with heads held high.

One by one the columns march onto Whitehall and halt in line ready for the service, engaging in inter service banter until God Save the Queen is played. There are immense crowds there to join in the service and to pay respect to the veterans and the fallen. Their applause once the march is underway is very moving and overwhelmingly emotional. At 11am the field guns mark the start and finish of the two minutes' silence following which The Queen lays a wreath and leaves. Then follows wreath laying by members of the Royal Family, military, ambassadors and other dignitaries after which they all leave Whitehall. Then the bands strike up with a military march and the march past begins.

Column by column we march past the Cenotaph performing an eyes left in tribute to the fallen and then on around the route until back at Horse Guards. We pass a second saluting base just before the finish of the march then go onto the parade ground to await the arrival of the last column of marchers. It's then back onto the coach for the drive back to the hotel where we have lunch, say our farewells and promise to meet again the following year.

Forty Six

IN 1986, the regiment was expanded taking in Royal Marines and Royal Engineer Parachutists. I continued my duties as the Quartermaster, keeping fit and leading a normal life. I was entitled to a war pension (for injured personnel) but I could not draw it whilst getting a service salary. I worked out how much I was losing, resigned my regular commission and became an officer in the Territorial Army. This meant I could draw a TA salary and my war pension together. I became the Permanent Staff Administrative Officer (PSAO) for two of the regiment's four reserve squadrons (there were four active regular squadrons) and still in bomb disposal. Previously I had been looking after all eight squadrons, working very long days, so this way I had more time with my daughters who were now attending senior school.

In many ways they were typical teenagers but they were well behaved, had part-time jobs and visited the old people living in the village, helping where they could. Around this time, due to something that had happened in Northern Ireland, I had personal protection. I told my children never to touch any parcels that the postman left. I would collect them myself. I ingrained it into my children that if we went to the beach they were not to pick anything up but to leave it alone and come and tell me.

Before this role, my office in the Bomb Disposal Unit at Lodge Hill was on the ground floor and my desk flanked a large window that faced onto the adjoining road. One day whilst sitting at my desk and using the telephone, there was a tremendous crash and a man holding onto a short ladder fell onto my desk together with most of the window frame and glass. I was petrified, but being a stony faced individual this didn't show. The man was obviously frightened but unhurt.

"Do you always call without an appointment?" I said and, shaking inwardly, I carried on with my telephone call. The man was employed by the contract window cleaners and was later heard telling his workmates what happened and that it was true that bomb disposal men had nerves of steel. If only he had known the truth!

At one point the unit deployed on NATO exercise, so my mother came to stay to care for the girls. It was a gruelling time with much night movement in Belgium. This was a major exercise during which many United Kingdom based units were exercised in their war time roles. After some days my artificial limb began to chafe my knee quite badly so I went to the casualty reception centre. Without explaining that I was an amputee, I asked for some Micropore tape to cover some blisters.

"Look, Sir, this unit was deployed from the UK equipped to deal with real casualties. If you came in with a hand or something missing I could help you." Without a word I sat down, removed my limb – complete with boot – and handed it to him. I was given the tape.

I received notification that I had been selected for the Man of the Men of the Years' Award, this being for a Man of the Year who further distinguishes himself. The presentation was again at the Savoy Hotel in London. On arrival we were met by Brian Johnson, "Johnners" of cricket commentary fame, and the press who wanted photographs for the evening papers. When I was chatting to Johnners, I noticed that his facial expression change but I didn't know why until I read the Evening Standard.

"Major Hambrook was standing on my foot. It was painful as he has a wooden leg you know."

During the pre-dinner reception I was chatting to a lady when I saw, across the room, Sir John Mills. I have always enjoyed his films so I said to the lady, "Please excuse me, as I would like to speak to John Mills."

"Oh," she said. "Tell him he must speak to you. I'm his wife."

Later that evening it was Sir John who made the presentation to me, reading my citation and presenting me with a beautiful decanter.

❖ ❖ ❖

THE LEEDS MEN OF THE YEAR'S DINNER

The Royal Association for Disability and Rehabilitation
25 Mortimer Street. London WIN SAB
Telephone: O1-637 5400

PATRON HER MAJESTY QUEEN ELIZABETH THE
QUEEN MOTHER

THE LEEDERS AWARDS
1990 MEN OF THE YEARS' DINNER
THURSDAY, 19 APRIL 1990

Major Stephen Hambrook GM

In recognition of his energy and perseverance in his fund-raising activities for RADAR and other charities.

In January 1983, Major Hambrook was badly injured by an exploding mine while serving in the Falklands. In December 1983 he marched 10 miles to raise money for the Canterbury Hospice and in August 1989 he raised over 4 thousand pounds for RADAR by going on a marathon trek in the Chichester International Cross Country March despite the pain walking causes him due to the injuries to both legs and an amputated foot. The event was a daunting 25 miles long which he completed in a time of 5 hours and 52 minutes and was an inspiration to many of the other marchers.

Major Hambrook received the George Medal for gallantry and was made a Man of the Year in 1970 and in 1987 received the Frankland-Moore Award for his work with disabled ex-servicemen. A block of flats built on the site where he defused a World War II bomb in Kentish Town is named Hambrook Court in honour of Stephen.

Stephen, a sensitive man who deeply cares for others, perseveres in his selfless service to disabled people and others needing help in his community. He is arranging the auction of a football, signed by the Gillingham Football Club Team (the Gills) and a cricket bat, signed by the 1989 County of Kent Cricket Team. These Mike Mahoney of Radio Kent will auction during his Cash for Charity programme.

RADAR Chairman His Grace The Duke of Buccleilch KT

The Leeds Men of the Years' Dinner Chairman The Right Honourable The Viscount Tonypandy PC DCL

RADAR Director George Wilson CBE

The regiment was undergoing another reorganisation and the unit I was with would be renamed and relocated near Royal Tunbridge Wells. It was a considerable distance from my home and as I was approaching my 60th birthday, had lost a foot but served for a further 10 years, the last six as a Permanent Staff Officer with a Territorial Army Bomb Disposal Unit, I decided to retire. I had served for 39 years. I was offered continuation on a yearly basis but I resigned my TA commission and entered civilian life in Tyler Hill.

My leaving report read:

> Major Hambrook has been 591 EOD Squadron's PSAO for over 6 years during which it developed into a well structured and manned unit of which its personnel are justly proud. He is an excellent PSAO with a thorough grasp of his duties, an outstanding ability to support both officers, and other ranks, in a quiet unobtrusive manner. This supportive attitude is extended to all within the regiment. He has a dry sense of humour and willingly helps those of lesser experience. A unit accounts computer package which he developed has been approved by the RAPC for others to use. His knowledge of

EOD and military matters is extensive. This he puts to the best possible use giving technical advice and input on all matters put to him, often doing so in a confidential manner which ensures credit will go to others. He is intelligent and quick of thought.

The contacts Major Hambrook has with MoD and other public information outlets are invaluable in his constant promotion of the TA and unit, recently returning voluntarily from leave to help produce an Options For Change brochure for SETAVRA (South East Territorial Auxiliary Volunteer Reserve Association). Encouraged by Major Hambrook, 591 Squadron has acquired a reputation for charitable giving with many thousands of pounds raised, the last being £800 for the County Air Ambulance Appeal.

591 Squadron is to be part of the reformed 221 Squadron. Major Hambrook has not sought to secure his own future but throughout has done what is best for the new unit. He is extremely loyal to his superiors, peers and subordinates but this is not always appreciated by those who do not know him well. Over the years since resigning from the regular forces until 2013, he, at various times, became involved in local and county community activities. He quietly undertakes much community work, supports and helps those less fortunate than he, and often represents individuals in their dealings with welfare matters.

Holder of the MBE, (Military Division) GM, LS&GC medal, GSM (NI). GOCs Commendation for Gallantry, twice a Man of The Year, actively involved in welfare and charity work. All in all, he is an outstanding man of the highest principles.

Forty Seven

IT WAS in 1991, and much to my surprise, that I was awarded
a MBE (Military Division). My daughter, Daniell, who was
working for a local paper wrote the following article about our
visit to the palace.

◈ ◈ ◈

On Tuesday 29 October, 1991, we all got up early. My dad,
sister Samantha and I were off to London to see The Queen,
well almost. Dad was going to see her to be made a Member of
The British Empire (Military Division). He had been appointed
in The Queen's Birthday Honours List 1991. We were going
to watch.

At 7.15am, David who was our driver for the day, arrived
at our house in a sparkling Montego which the army had lent
us for the occasion. David knew the way to London and to
Buckingham Palace as he had taken others from the Bomb
Disposal Regiment – just as well as Dad was too nervous to
drive as well as he thinks he normally does.

The journey up was fairly slow due to traffic. Sam and I
slept most of the way while Dad worried about which part of
his uniform he had left at home. In the event he hadn't! It was
all safely in the boot of the car. For security reasons the cars
cannot be identifiable as military vehicles and the occupants
must wear civilian clothes.

We arrived at about 10.15am and the police parked us in the Mall to wait for the opening of the gates at 10.30am. Soon after, we were directed into the inner quadrangle along with a number of other cars and again parked where we were shown. There was an anxious moment whilst we were going in. Two policemen were checking the car while another checked our invitations. We had our tickets handy and David had the car pass but Dad had put his letter of invitation into his jacket pocket and the jacket was in the car boot. Eventually, we were in and waited while Dad put on the other bits of his uniform.

Once ready we walked to the entrance. Just inside Sam and I were directed along a red carpet and up a flight of stairs along the length of which were stationed bodyguards resplendent in plumed helmets and shining breastplates complete with swords in hand. My Dad was whipped off to another place, not that it mattered as we found him at the top of the stairs looking for the loo – just can't take ones parents anywhere! He presumably found the cloakroom while we were being taken into the palace ballroom where the investiture was to take place. Our seats were quite close to the dais where The Queen was to be. All this was to the strains of the Guards band which was playing from the ballroom balcony. It is a beautiful room, lovely crystal chandeliers and royal style decor, hard to remember and describe as so much was happening at once especially as it was important to see what the other women were wearing. It's easy for the men – uniform or if not in the services, a morning suit – but difficult for us. Those to receive medals etc, were in the Palace Art Gallery being sorted into order and advised on what to do and when. The atmosphere was remarkably relaxed and the palace staff did everything they could to ensure that it was a happy event for all.

At precisely 11am the band played God Save The Queen as Queen Elizabeth, together with her entourage and a guard of Beefeaters, entered the ballroom and the investitures began. She seemed smaller and more petite than we had imagined and looked just lovely. It was the first time either of us had been so close to her. Each presentation was made individually and The Queen had a smile and something to say to each person whilst pinning on their medals, then she shook their hand before they moved on through a side passage to seats in the centre of the ballroom where they sat to watch the rest of the presentations.

We were a bit worried as after shaking hands with The Queen, the award recipient has to walk backwards about six steps before bowing, turning to the right and heading for the side passage. Dad can do lots with his artificial leg, almost anything but walk backwards! Had he fallen he would have pretended to have fainted or something like that, but the excuse wasn't needed as he managed quite well.

When all of the presentations had been made the band again played the national anthem while The Queen and her procession left the ballroom. Then all mingled as the heroes and relatives tried to find each other. We met and spoke to Dad and agreed to meet at the car as he was anxious to avoid the press and TV who were waiting at the foot of the stairs. He remembered a side exit that he had used before and having collected his hat did a bunk to the car.

David was waiting for us with a big smile on his face as he had just met the England rugby coach who was made an OBE. We then had a quick reversal of roles as Dad used David's camera to take photos of Dave with the palace as a background – Dad's nice like that.

Then it was into the car and out through the crowd at the gate on our way back. Suddenly Dad shouted, "Stop Dave!" and leapt out of the car into the crowd. He had seen his brother, Ken, who by coincidence was working in London. Scattering people either way, he ploughed through to say hello and have a chat. We almost became the first car to be rammed from the rear in a palace gate!

Soon we were on our way to a pub in Chatham where Dad's work mates had arranged a lunch for us. We slept most of the way there while the men chatted. On arrival, the smell of food woke us up. Well, it had been eight hours since we had anything to eat or drink. It was a lovely, very happy meal during which Dad was given an inscribed pen and pencil set. He was much moved and has since hidden them so that we can't borrow them.

What more can I say about a day like this? Not much as it was so exciting and out of this world that the detail is difficult to remember. What more can we say about a Dad like ours, except that he is ours, that he loves us as we do him and he is always there when we need him. That's why he gets presents on both Mother's and Father's Day. Why, you may ask did he get yet another medal? Well, we tried asking but he only grinned and said, 'It was for putting up with you!'

We are very proud of the medals he has and he is always very modest about them. However, browsing through the scrapbooks, I found that Dad got the George Medal for a very large bomb in London and two others elsewhere (and had a block of flats named after him), a medal for service in Northern Ireland, a Commendation for gallantry when serving in a diving unit, another medal for service, was a Man of the Year in 1971 and Man of the Men of the Year in 1990. Since he was injured in the Falklands he has been helping disabled people in his spare time; for this he was given a national award in 1987. Part of that citation read, 'He is a sensitive man who deeply cares for others and he perseveres in his selfless service to disabled people and others in his community needing help. In all, he is a most remarkable man.'

◈ ◈ ◈

When I got the MBE, Mum sent me a telegram and it read, "Dear Stevie, first the GM, now the MBE. We're so proud of you. Love, Mum."

I had been fortunate in that at both of my investitures – the George Medal and my MBE – it was The Queen who presented them to me. I have also, on four occasions, been a guest at the Buckingham Palace garden party. Once was to celebrate the 75th anniversary of the formation of the British Limbless Ex-Service Men's Association.

A number of members were selected to be introduced to The Queen and I was honoured to be among them. It was a memorable day.

Before The Queen makes her entrance at the party one is free, along with about two thousand or more other guests, to explore the magnificent gardens, listen at leisure to a military band and enjoy the delicate refreshments. Just before The Queen appears, the ushers get the guests into some sort of order then the national anthem is played as The Queen leaves the Palace to stand at the top of the steps. When the anthem has finished The Queen and her entourage come down the steps to meet her guests and stay for about an hour following which the national anthem is again played and The Queen leaves the garden for the palace. The guests then slowly disperse having enjoyed a wonderful event.

In 2011, I was invited to present a prize on behalf of the charity Help for Heroes at a dinner to be held in the Savoy Hotel. The event was extremely well attended, possibly 50 circular tables with 10 guests sat at each. The newscaster Katie Derham was the presenter. I was seated at a table with Rick Jolly, the Royal Marine Senior Medical Officer during the Falklands conflict who had written a book of his experiences titled The Red And Green Life Machine. He gave me a signed copy. Together we were to present an award to the Virgin Atlantic airline which had been named the most efficient in the travel business. After a pleasant lunch the awards ceremony started. I had my back to the stage on which there was a large screen and one of the people at our table suddenly said to me, "Is that you?" I turned and saw a short clip of me working on a bomb from the Seven Seconds To Run film. Then Katie read out the following citation:

◈ ◈ ◈

"On October 1, 1969, Stephen was part of a bomb disposal team deployed to defuse a World War II bomb discovered in Camden, London. It was surrounded by houses, blocks of flats and railway lines. Due to the instability of the explosives, the device had to be rendered safe by hand. Stephen and his colleague discovered the bomb had a triggering timer set for 17 seconds which had jammed after seven – a mere 10 seconds were left to run. If the clock restarted, they would have only three seconds to attempt to choke off the fuze mechanism and then seven seconds to get clear.

'I sometimes wonder,' his colleague said later, 'if anything went wrong, whether we would see a blinding flash or if one knows nothing at all.'

The whole operation took 29 hours, 11 of these under extreme danger. Stephen was awarded the George Medal for his selfless courage and dedication.

During the Falklands War in 1982, Argentine forces laid thousands of mines and in the wake of the conflict, Stephen was deployed to the Falkland Islands to command the team clearing Argentine mines. During the difficult and complex operations, a mine detonated severing the lower part of his leg. Stephen recovered to serve another 10 years. Since 1983 he has acted as a volunteer welfare representative looking after the needs of servicemen and women who have lost limbs. He was awarded a MBE, military division, in 1991."

Forty Eight

ONCE retired, I began teaching information technology up to Open University level at a local college, Maidstone Category C men's prison and East Sutton Park prison – an open prison for women working toward their release. I also became a primary school governor and into my computing class one day came a mother of a child at that school. To her distress I recognised her. She told me that her son had been told that she was in hospital, not prison. I assured her that I would not betray her secret and so it remained.

Teaching was an interesting experience and quite well paid. I did it for nearly three years until the college changed the terms of the contract, introducing a basic salary and not paying travel costs, which made the job not worth having. While teaching in Maidstone Prison I visited one pupil during the official visiting hour. While we were chatting one of the notorious Kray twins, Reggie, came into the visiting hall. He was an inmate but walked like a confident royal expecting adulation, moving through the tables, stopping here and there to shake a hand, until he reached our table and reached for me.

"No," I said.

"Why?" he asked.

"Because I choose whose hand I shake," I replied. The inmate I was visiting was very fearful of a violent reaction but Kray just snorted and moved away.

It seemed quite natural to me that after I left the regular army I should become more involved in community work since I had always regarded my bomb disposal work as a service to the community anyway. What I had not foreseen was how, once you volunteer for one post, others follow in quite quick succession – even if some only require one to attend quarterly meetings. From the time I resigned from the regular forces to 2013 I was a parish councillor and parish council chairman, a school governor and deanery councillor. I joined the Kent Rural Community Management Committee, the Kent Rural Community Halls Committee and the Canterbury Association of Parish Councils Executive Committee. At the Tyler Hill Memorial Hall I was the secretary for three years, then treasurer, all alongside my work for BLESMA. Many of these appointments led to others which would run alongside or intermingle with each other. I was as busy as I had been at work, perhaps even more so.

What was interesting and surprising was the difference in attitude between myself and those who have never served in the Armed Forces. I was used to the military way of working where if the committee made a decision and some were against it, but the majority was for it, then all members supported the final decision. At Tyler Hill Memorial Hall I discovered that those who had disagreed originally would then go on to try and sway other trustees into their way of thinking.

It was at the nearby Blean Primary School that I became the local authority representative governor on the governing board. Over time I chaired the buildings sub-committee, became vice-chair and then chairman of governors. It was in the main an enjoyable experience and I served until 2013 when acute illness – chronic obstructive pulmonary disease and asbestosis, both as a result of my work with explosives – and the amputation of my right leg below the knee forced me to stand down.

I was involved at Blean for 23 years and during my time there I formed the school golf club. We had about 25 members. The school had a large playing field and at first we used donated adult clubs that I cut down. When the club was established with the weekly session being led by a club assistant professional, the youngsters began to progress and I bought sufficient junior clubs. These were sold to me by a professional at Chestfield Golf Club at a generous discount.

We also had occasional Saturday sessions at the golf club using the practise ground. Some of the pupils became junior members of the club which was pleasing. One amusing incident was during a training session when a club hit my artificial leg. I hadn't told the children about my leg and one of the young boys said, "Mister, you're scared of us ain't yer?"

"What do you mean?" I said.

"Cos' you're wearing shin pads," came the reply.

I came to love golf when, in 1987, I went on a BLESMA golfing activity in Wales and decided to take it up as a relaxing hobby. Before I left Wales I spent some time with the club professional discussing the clubs that I would need. He was very good and advised me not to buy a driver and only a cheap putter as over time my gained experience would guide me to a correct choice. I was grateful to him for his help and returned to my home with golf clubs. I bought a golf practise net and mat, which was erected in my garden, where I practised most days. I also went to a local golf range and then decided to join a club. I visited and played at three clubs in Kent and decided to join the one which made me feel most welcome – Chestfield Golf Club about six miles from my home. I remained a full playing member until 2012 when, after a bout of severe illnesses and the loss of my right leg under the knee due to a hospital acquired infection, I was unable to walk let alone play, so I changed my membership to social.

I became aware that there were many clubs and activities going on in the Tyler Hill Memorial Hall. I thought that it would be good to let the wider community know about them, as well as other things, so in 1992, I started the Tyler Hill Community Magazine. This was published in booklet form four times a year and delivered free of charge to all the homes in the village. It was produced by a team and printed professionally. I found a co-editor who proof read it, and a treasurer and advertising manager. We formed a management committee, remaining as such until the final edition in the summer of 2013. During that time the magazine received two awards and was also granted the status of Community Champion by the Department of Education and Skills. Any monies raised through the advertising were used to offset the cost of printing and various community projects such as free CVs for people in the village who were out of work. We also provided and fitted security window sashes and locks for the local older population.

In 1992, the Daily Telegraph published an article promoting a Royal Yacht Association scheme. Organisations could hire a fleet of six trailer mounted dinghies suitable for youngsters, to teach them how to sail. I enjoyed working with young people and while in Sittingbourne had run the cub pack at the local church. Having contacted the RYA representative and booked them for a week, I spoke to the owners of a large lake at nearby Westbere and got permission to use it and got the resident sailing club to agree to our use of the clubhouse. Some experienced sailors volunteered to act as instructors and safety boat crews. Once again The Queen was helpful in providing two 4-tonne army trucks for a fortnight twice a year. And once again I am sure she would have been delighted had she known.

I applied for and obtained funding from the Kent Community Foundation for the hire of the dinghies and other various expenses and then advertised the free event for up to 12 trainees aged eight to 12. Priority was given to those who were disadvantaged in any way, or for whatever reason would not get a holiday. Over the years the young volunteers were trained by the RYA in various duties. The Tyler Hill community magazine paid for this until ultimately we became self-sufficient in instructors (youngsters who had benefitted and returned to volunteer) and safety crews.

For the last six years of the sailing, Kent County Council made community grants. This covered most of the costs with the remainder paid from magazine funds. The true success of the venture was down to the volunteers who started as trainees and then returned over the years bringing happiness to many youngsters – 240 in total – while becoming sailors of distinction themselves. The last event was in 2012 when due to my health I was unable to continue to organise and participate in these activities and they were, sadly, discontinued.

When I was doing the sailing courses with the children, some of them asked me about my leg. I told them that I had been diving a wreck and seen a shoal of sharks nearby. I explained that I waited for them to swim away but they hadn't and I was worried I would run out of air. The only solution was to grit my teeth and stick my foot out of a hole. My hope being that one shark would take my foot and the others would chase it. The sharks behaved as expected and I was free to swim to the surface. One of the mums came and spoke to me, "Is that completely true?" she said.

"No," I said. "I didn't like to tell them about the other divers I pushed out first."

A BBC television programme made for schools about the Second World War highlighted various events and included the footage of the Chalk Farm incident which had been updated to say that I had been awarded the George Medal and, some years later, had stepped on a mine in the Falklands.

My granddaughter Catherine, having seen it at school with her friends, rang me and said "Granddad, you're a pig. You told me it was a shark and I told all my friends!"

Forty Nine

WHILE I was still working and after Gill left, it became obvious that my daughters needed something other than me to share their affection and after much consideration I decided we should get a dog and found a local breeder. She had a litter of shorthaired Labradors for sale. We went to her kennels and saw six pups – one with dark brown eyes.

"You wouldn't want that one as you wouldn't be able to show him," she said. But of course that was the one the girls immediately fell for. We couldn't get close to the puppies as they were not fully inoculated and hadn't been weaned but we paid a deposit. The breeder had to come and see our home to ensure we were suitable for her thoroughbred dogs and I had to agree to her rules as to how we would bring the dog up for the first two years, including agreeing to the lady making occasional visits. She added that if we wanted the dog to be obedient we should also get a cat and it so happened that my Commanding Officer's wife had a cat which had just given birth to a litter. She agreed that I could have one when they were weaned.

During the waiting period of about three weeks I told my daughters that they needed elocution lessons. They were not very happy about it and when the day came to collect the cat, I told them we were going to meet their elocution teacher. I drove them to the house and when the door opened the girls stomped in with very long faces. I quickly and quietly explained to the woman and she left the room, returning with a lovely kitten. How quickly the girls' mood changed when they realised the cat was theirs to take home although they rebuked me for winding them up. The cat, which we named Harriet, quickly settled in and a few days later our dog came home too. Because of his lion-like eyes, and because we thought it was very original, we decided to call him Zimba. But on our first walk through the nearby fields we met another dog – also called Zimba.

One day I went to visit a BLESMA member. He was almost totally incapable and as I had Zimba in the car, I asked the man's wife if I could bring the young dog in. She agreed and Zimba went straight to the man's bed and sat down as if he had been trained to do so. The bedridden man reached out a hand, put it on Zimba's head and smiled. His wife was delighted as she said that was his first smile in months. From then on I took Zimba on all my visits and he behaved impeccably. Rather than leave him alone all day, I also took him to work where he became a favourite with the soldiers. They took him on patrol around camp and after a while his name was added to the unit personality board as K9 Warrant Officer Zimba. The relationship between Harriet, soon shortened to Harry, and Zimba was good but the cat was dominant and took to sharing the dog's basket, sometimes sleeping on his back or between his front paws, and when in the house generally stayed close to him. Zimba was never allowed upstairs, a rule he seemed to accept, but when I was upstairs in bed having contracted a severe bout of pleurisy and was laid low, I awoke to find him sitting by the bed with his head resting on my hand.

Fifty

A COMMON question that arose after I lost my foot was whether I would do this job again if I had my life over. The answer is that I would do everything exactly the same, because without the life I've had I wouldn't have the children and the wonderful family that I've got. My eldest son Stephen works in specialist engineering, Gareth is self-employed in building maintenance and Morris works for an international company providing business plans. My daughters have also successful careers. Sam is a Band 7 nursing sister specialising in critical care and Dani is a classroom assistant at a primary school.

I have nine grandchildren: Carl, Simon, Tara, Rio, Jake, Jessica, Hazel, Catherine and Karen. I enjoy being a grandpa even when they make remarks like Jake did when he saw a photograph of me in my younger days and said, "Granddad was good looking until he got all crackly."

I wouldn't say that losing part of my leg was life defining and I wouldn't want it to be how my life is defined to others. Once I got a leg that I could use, it just became part of my whole story, something in the mix. You've got to be philosophical. People much younger than me sit in wheelchairs and waste away. That's just not me. I did miss running a bit, as it wasn't only the physical element of it that I loved, but the mental relaxation. The only time I got upset about it was when I moved into Tyler Hill and the Kent half marathon went past.

Overall, I've enjoyed a good career. Do I like detonating things? I don't know. I've never thought about it. It gets rid of them safely, I suppose. I knew what bombs could do but to me, it was all a challenge and even though I have been badly injured, I am glad I've had the career I've had. Look at the places I've been. And I didn't have to pay any air fares! There is a sense of purpose to army life that suited me and today I have a pension that is funded by the community. I resolved to try to repay this by helping as and when, and where, I could.

My father died two years after I got back from the Falklands. He was young, only 70, and all the family was in touch with him. Mum died about a year after I got my MBE, she was 94. She had a fall and seemed to be recovering but went downhill unexpectedly. I was on my way to see her to talk about her having some respite care, when my brother rang to say I should get there as quickly as possible. I made it and she died soon afterwards. I was there at her bedside as were my brothers.

Ken was called up for National Service but didn't make the army his career. His national service seemed to go on forever because they would add another 14 days every time he did something wrong. He laughs about it to this day. Ken's a member of Shoreham Old Boys' Club and they have a reunion several times a year. He tells me there's a plaque on the wall in my honour. I will go along one year. But I always send my regards via my brother and they send theirs to me.

Peter is retired and enjoys paragliding, unfortunately his wife Audrey does not enjoy good health. Ken and his wife Rita play indoor bowls with Rita progressing to the National Finals. My younger brother Francis lives a quiet life with his dog.

I don't have any regrets. I am sorry that I may have caused some unhappiness to my wives. It's difficult to be married to someone who is there for breakfast then leaves for three weeks.

I didn't write a list of everything that I wanted from life but if I wrote one now, I think I could tick it all off. The thing I wanted most was a loving family and children of whom I am very proud. Happily, I have achieved this.

If I go to sleep and wake up tomorrow, I shall be content. If don't wake up, I shall be content. Life has been very good to me.

Stephen Hambrook, December 2014

Decorations and awards

1968   Commander in Chief (BAOR) Commendation for brave conduct

1970   The George Medal

1970   Army Man of the Year

1972   Long Service and Good Conduct Medal

1974   General Service Medal (Northern Ireland Clasp)

1987   BLESMA National Award

1990   Man of the Men of the Years' Award

1991   Appointed as a Member of the British Empire

2011   BLESMA National Award